MINDSET
TO
MILLIONAIRE

7 KEYS TO BECOMING A REAL ESTATE MILLIONAIRE

MITCH A. NELSON

Mitch A Nelson
www.MitchANelson.com
Email: mitchanelson@gmail.com

Published by:
Mitch A. Nelson
63 East 11400 South, #230
Sandy, UT 84070
Phone: (832) 572-5285
E-mail: info@EliteOnlinePublishing.com
Any source code or other supplementary materials referenced by the author of this text is available to readers at www.MitchANelson.com

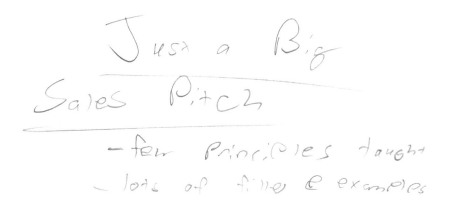

Just a Big
Sales Pitch

- few Principles taught
- lots of filler & examples

*To all the people who believed in me and
helped me make the transition from
employee to Millionaire.*

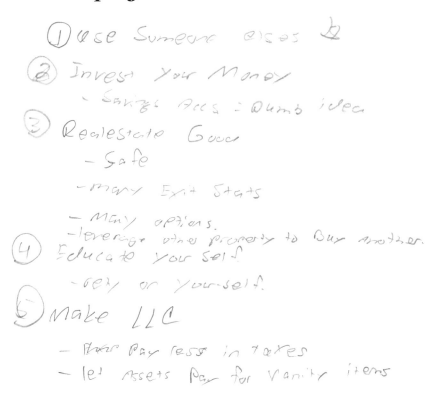

1. Use Someone else's $
2. Invest Your Money
   - Savings Acc = Dumb idea
3. Realestate Good
   - Safe
   - many Exit Stats
   - Many options.
   - leverage other property to Buy another.
4. Educate Your self
   - rely on yourself.
5. Make LLC
   - then Pay less in taxes
   - let Assets Pay for Vanity items

Contents

Contents i

Table of Figures iii

Preface v

About the Author vii

Introduction ix

1. Change Your Mindset: Get Out of the Employee Trap 1

2. Wealthy People Own Businesses 55

3. Wealthy People Invest 71

4. The Magic of Real Estate 85

5. Never Spend the First Dollar 95

6. Leverage and Good Debt VS Bad Debt 101

7. Education 123

About the Author 135

Table of Figures

Figure 1: Weathly Mindset VS Employee Mindset   2

Figure 2: Pillars of Wealth   7

Figure 3: My car, 2016 Z51 Stingray   9

Figure 4: Amortization Mortgage   14

Figure 5: Cost of 30 Year Mortgage   15

Figure 6: Maintain Drive   39

Figure 7: Think Outside the Box   43

Figure 8: Believe in Yourself   50

Figure 9: Success   55

Figure 10: Own a Business   59

Figure 11: Start your Business   61

Figure 12: Time to Invest   71

Figure 13: Farmer Allocation   74

Figure 14: Golden Egg   77

Figure 15: Invest in Yourself   82

Figure 16: Diversify your Investments   85

Figure 17: Leverage Real Estate   89

Figure 18: Equity is Fantastic   92

Figure 19: Real Estate is Magical   93

Figure 20: Money is not just a picture   96

Figure 21: Pay yourself first   97

Figure 22: Guy who gave first dollar   99

Figure 23: Difference between Bad Debt and Good Debt   102

Figure 24: Bad Debt   104

Figure 25: Debt   109

Figure 26: Example Amortization Schedule   120

Figure 27: Debt Categories   121

Figure 28: Education   123

Figure 29: Knowledge is Power   130

Figure 30: Education   133

Preface

Several years ago, I started out my career in sales; I worked in the print industry, and I was selling print advertising. The job was the typical day job, every day the same thing; I was on salary pay commission, and it was just a grind. I went to work every day and focused on making those sales, earning only a little extra commission with each one.

I was just barely paying the bills with the money I was bringing in. I started to realize very quickly that this routine was not what I wanted to do for the rest of my life. I was young, in my early 20s, and it became something that started gnawing at me. I began to think that I wanted to be wealthy, successful, and I want to enjoy what I do. I began looking at the people in my life that I knew were successful, and I asked myself, "What are these people doing differently?"

I noticed the most successful people I knew had an abundance of free time to go along with their abundance of money, and I asked what the secret was to their success. After a while, I started to realize there was a commonality in their behaviors, in the way they think, and in their mindset. I found that wealthy people own businesses, so I decided that's what I needed to do.

I started a web marketing business that became a quick success. As I have continued to grow as an entrepreneur, I've come to realize that the wealthy are not just business owners.

The wealthy own businesses and invest in real estate. My intention with this book is to give those who know there is more for them – those who long for true wealth and prosperity in their lives, a guide to help them take their first steps toward being wealthy.

My goal and the reason why I started coaching is I want to help people. I want to facilitate and educate them on how to become wealthy. There really is freedom in changing your mindset. I believe many people out there are just like me, and the grind is not for them. I want to bridge the gap between the mentality of working for someone, building *their* wealth, and trading your time for money; versus working for yourself, having employees and creating more time and money for yourself.

This can be accomplished through owning businesses and investing your money wisely. This gap between a **Wealthy Mindset** and an **Employee Mindset** is real and can be a struggle; my purpose for this book is to teach people how to build a bridge between these two mindsets and succeed.

About the Author

For over 10 years, Mitch Nelson has enjoyed starting, running and investing in businesses and real estate. Like many of his companies, he has thrived in business taking on each new challenge it brings. From the printing industry to service and retail, as well as information and technology companies, Mitch's portfolio of influence as an entrepreneur is well known throughout the Rocky Mountain region. His hands-on experience in many corners of business is a trusted resource for his colleagues and investors alike.

One of Mitch's most exciting business ventures has been that of real estate investing. With his years of experience, he's learned to navigate and make money in the real estate realm while learning to avoid pitfalls and traps that claim many young investors. He has dedicated much of his time to teaching others his techniques and passing on his secrets of the industry through writing, videos, coaching and education programs. Contact Mitch A. Nelson at:

Email: mitchanelson@gmail.com

Web: www.MitchANelson.com

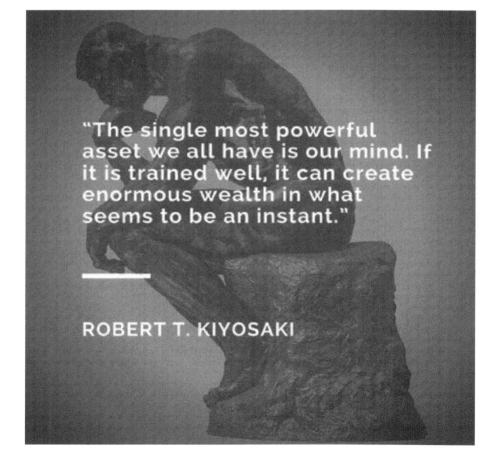

Introduction

Mindset to Millionaire: 7 Keys to Becoming a Real Estate Millionaire. Don't learn the hard way and utilize the steps outlined in this book to change your mindset from an employee to a Millionaire

The author, Mitch A. Nelson, started as an employee with an entrepreneur mind. He didn't want to work 9 to 5 and just be good enough. He wanted more and studied and determined the best methods to make this transition. Mitch shares his knowledge of real estate investing to help you get started.

The chapters are formatted to be followed in order, or each chapter can stand on its own with information applicable to that concept of *Mindset to Millionaire*. The whole book is about how to change this mindset to realize unlimited wealth.

Chapter 1 introduces a concept of changing your mindset and getting the feel of not being an employee. Not getting stuck in the 9 to 5 trap. A shift in mindset can be profitable and help your business get started or stay profitable if you consider the options. There are two types of mindsets when it comes to money: *Employee Mindset* and *Wealthy Mindset*.

Chapter 1 also introduces the *Pillars of Wealth*. The four pillars are *Tax, Velocity Banking Strategy (VBS),*

Business and *Real Estate.* You must keep and build on these pillars to obtain wealth.

Chapter 2 describes the second key of **Mindset to Millionaire** which is to own a business. Wealthy people own one or more businesses.

Chapter 3 introduces the *third* key of **Mindset to Millionaire** which is *investing.*

Chapter 4 describes the roadmap of making real estate a great investment strategy by explaining the *fourth* key of **Mindset to Millionaire** is to *diversify your investments.*

Chapter 5 introduces how to utilize your money options to make the most of them. The *fifth* key to **Mindset to Millionaire** is explained as never spending the first dollar. People in the **Employee Mindset** have their paycheck come in and what's the first thing they do with it? They give it to other people.

Chapter 6 explains how to leverage your money. The *sixth* key to **Mindset to Millionaire** is *Leverage,* and this chapter starts by clarifying the difference between an asset and liability.

Chapter 7 discusses strategy and provides the best way to get started utilizing education. I have personal experiences in that chapter to inform you of mistakes not to make.

Mindset to Millionaire*: 7 Keys to Becoming a Real Estate Millionaire* helps you understand the steps required to begin becoming a *Millionaire.*

To get updates on this book
and access a FREE
Millionaire Mindset Checklist
text your
Name and Email to

1 (801) 666-4776

or visit

www.MitchANelson.com.

You can also schedule a
consulting session.

xii

Chapter 1

Change Your Mindset: Get Out of the Employee Trap

The *first* key to the book **Mindset to Millionaire** is to change your mindset.   Mindset is the primary factor in obtaining financial freedom and success.   Change your thoughts, achieve the results you want to achieve, and embrace the future you imagined.

There are two types of mindsets when it comes to money: **Employee Mindset** and **Wealthy Mindset**. To change your mindset from an **Employee Mindset** to a **Wealthy Mindset** you need to habitually create a shift in your mindset and expand your thoughts to encompass the ideas of new opportunity and risk. The change will be uncomfortable at first, but you will relax once you start receiving great rewards from your success.

WEALTHY MINDSET VS EMPLOYEE MINDSET

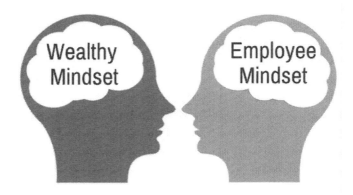

Figure 1: Weathly Mindset VS Employee Mindset

The ***Employee Mindset*** encompasses the axiom that everybody has heard before *"Money doesn't grow on trees."* The ***Employee Mindset*** looks something like this: you save your money, work hard, go to school, earn a degree, and with that degree, you get a great job, and that's that.

There is not a lot of upsides to being an employee, but time is the great equalizer. It's the only thing that everybody has in common. I have 24 hours in a day; you have 24 hours in a day, Donald Trump has 24 hours in a day; regardless of how rich or poor we all are, that's all the hours we have in a day.

As an employee, you must be physically present to get paid. If you've got this sort of job, then you're trading your time for money. You must show up, you must do your work, and you get paid for your time and work. If that's what you want, there's nothing wrong with that, but if that's not what you want, then there is something wrong. You need to change your mindset and think more like a wealthy person.

You need to shift from an Employee Mindset to a Wealthy Mindset.

The retirement plan of the ***Employee Mindset*** involves a plan, called the "***40, 40, 40 Plan***." Here are some interesting statistics about the "***40, 40, 40 Plan***":

- **95%** of people are dead, disabled, or financially broke by the age of **67**
- **54%** of those people are dependent, which means they rely on a child or on an assisted-living type scenario
- **36%** are still working by the time they are **65**. This is the plan for a lot of people now, to just keep working.
- **4%** of people are financially independent, which in most cases means that their 401k can provide for all their retirement needs.

Most people in this group worked the "***40, 40, 40 Plan***" and the company they worked for matched their financial contribution to their 401k retirement plan. They didn't borrow any money out of it over the years and have accrued enough money to be financially independent.

The last **1%** is the wealthy, or what I call the **Wealthy Mindset**. I will get into more about the difference between rich and wealthy later in this book, but the **1%** of the population is wealthy because their money is creating more wealth for them. Their money hires employees and makes money for them.

When people trade their time for money to pay the bills, they have much less money to invest. The wealthy don't think that way. The wealthy exchange their money for money, but they also trade their money for time. Wealthy people get paid while they sleep, whereas employees don't. The wealthy can use their incoming money to pay their monthly bills and not even touch their savings.

What does this concept look like in real dollars? If you're 20 years from retirement, and you'd like to retire on $7,500 per month; you'll need to save $2.5 million, and have almost $2.6 million in your retirement account. Currently, $7500 might seem like a lot of money to an elderly couple who are empty-nesters now, but for someone 20 years from now, inflation is factored in.

Twenty years ago, $4000 a month would have provided a comfortable living for a retired couple. Twenty years ago, $4000 seemed like a lot of money; and so two decades from now, $7500, which seems like a lot of money now, is not going to be enough for a comfortable living.

The retirement plan mentioned above probably seems overwhelming, and you may be thinking there's not a light at the end of the tunnel; or if there is, it's a very dim light, but the light at the end of the tunnel comes when you change your **Employee Mindset** to a **Wealthy Mindset**.

It's the wealthy who have businesses and invest, who get paid dividends even while they sleep, vacation, or travel. The wealthy simply breathe and make money. Truly wealthy people develop the habits and techniques to make money, but the first step is changing your mindset.

> ### *Wealthy people value their time more than their money.*

If you think about it in terms of renewable resources, money is something that you can always make more of: time is not. The wealthy create businesses and invest, trading their money for time (rather than their time for money – like employees do). They're trading the renewable resource for the non-renewable one.

> ## *The real key to building real wealth and keeping it, is changing your mindset.*

Changing your mindset is the secret to earning money in your sleep and gaining more time to do those things you really want to do.

PILLARS OF WEALTH

My most valuable concept I can teach you is called the ***Pillars of Wealth.*** Pillars are used as a support for a building, and I metaphorically represent pillars as a support for your transition from the ***Employee Mindset*** to a ***Wealthy Mindset***.

Keeping and building wealth is easy once you have the correct principles and practices in place. The challenge is the mindset shift. You must live and breathe your shift to a ***Wealthy Mindset***. You need to believe that you are worthy of wealth and success. You must visualize yourself with wealth, and all that wealth can bring to make your life easier.

With this book, I want to teach you a solution to keep and build wealth. I developed the ***Pillars of Wealth*** to provide a map, or blueprint, on how to keep and build wealth.

I am successful. Why not do the steps I do, the same way I do and obtain wealth.

The first two pillars of the **Pillars of Wealth** represent how to **keep** wealth. These two pillars are **Tax** and my **Velocity Banking Strategy (VBS)**. The last two pillars are how to **build** wealth and include **Business** and **Real Estate**. This concept is illustrated in the following figure:

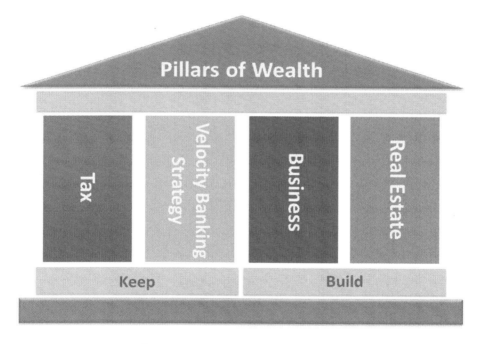

Figure 2: Pillars of Wealth

Going from the **Employee Mindset** to the **Wealthy Mindset** is going to require some sacrifices. I have a personal example to share about how to use the **Pillars of Wealth** to make money to buy your dream purchase.

THE FIRST PILLAR IS TAX.

Tax demonstrates that the average employee pays more taxes because they do what they were taught. If you're an independent contractor, you get a 1099 form from an employer. If you're an employee, you receive a W-2. The W-2 is the most expensive way to pay taxes.

The employee pays **34%** of their income in interest, a **33%** in taxes, and the last **33%** is theirs to keep. While the wealthy person, only pays **5%** in taxes.

I recently purchased my dream car, a 2016 Chevrolet Corvette Z51 Stingray. This is a $100,000 car, and I would not have been able to purchase this car if I was an employee working for someone else.

> *The reason I could buy this car is I do not leverage my time I leverage the Pillars of Wealth.*

Figure 3: My car, 2016 Z51 Stingray

The **Pillars of Wealth** allowed me to buy a $100,000 car. Yes, that is right! **A $100,000 CAR!!!!** Most Americans buy a car worth $25,000, but I made my dream come true by utilizing the **Pillars of Wealth**.

The car was $98,000 out the door. Using pillar one, **Tax**, I utilized a tax law for business miles that says if I use the car for advertising, I can deduct business miles.

I put a sign on the back windshield with company contact information. I get to write off the trip I make to my parents' house for Sunday dinner as advertising as well as a visit to my most recent *Fix-N-Flip* project. The advertising of my business allows me to deduct all the mileage anywhere I go. I get to write off that amount using this strategy.

> ## *Every mile I drive I deduct for advertising.*

Whether I am driving for business or driving regularly, it doesn't matter because I am advertising wherever I go. I write off the current business mileage rate of **53.5** cents per mile. I have owned the car three months, and it currently has *8100* miles.

If I multiply 8100 * .535, I get the total of my current deduction which is $4,333.5. That is the amount I can deduct so far, this year. I have paid two car payments of $1,700. I have paid a total of $3,400, and I can write off $4,600. By the time I pay the third payment, I will have utilized Pillar One, **Tax**, to purchase the car of my dreams.

> ## *Pillar one pays for my car. Every single year!*

THE SECOND PILLAR IS VELOCITY BANKING STRATEGY (VBS)

MAD is a way to leverage your debt to create more wealth. The average person's financial structure is set up the way the bank has told them to set it up.

The average American employee makes about **$40,000** a year or **$3,500** a month. The interest the average American pays is to a bank. The Bank is not going to tell you to do something that is good for you they are going to tell you what is good for the Bank. They are making more money from us than we are making from them.

The Employee Mindset person does not take the time to figure out how their money is working.

The **Employee Mindset** person is told to put all their money into the bank with money going to both checking and savings. We are taught from childhood to **save money**. You are trained to think that your savings is your emergency fund, and you cannot touch it.

The banks want you to think that you should save money. The banks are using the money from every member's savings accounts to loan out money. For example, you have $10,000 in savings; you want to buy a car for $8,000.

The bank suggests you obtain a loan for the car to build your credit and they charge you **6%** interest. The bank then borrows the money from your savings account to loan to you.

The bank is paying **0.2%** interest on your savings, and you are paying **6%** interest on your loan. Who is winning?

Can you pay cash for your house?

The **Employee Mindset** says no. It sounds like a mortgage is the only option. Mortgages are the most expensive lending option in existence.

The **Wealthy Mindset** looks at a typical Mortgage model **6%** APR and sees its measured on a different scale, for example, the freezing temperature point of water is 32°F and 0°C. They are different numbers, yet they are the same temperature and even measured in the same unit of measurement, degrees, just measured on different scales.

The **Employee Mindset** sees the advertised **6%** APR Mortgage as more attractive than **21%** APR. Lower rates always look better in the **Employee Mindset** thinking.

The **Wealthy Mindset** sees something different. Let me explain, mortgages are always *Amortized Interest*. The banks will still amortize if they can.

What makes amortized loans so great for the bank?

Is that they get the front load of interest first. The banks use the excuse that you are a risk, even when they have your house as collateral.

> ### *The bank will always take their profit first.*

So let's take a *$200,000* Mortgage. The bank loans you *$200,000* with a *6%* Annual Percentage Rate (APR) Interest. Your first Mortgage payment is *$1000*. *$950* is for Interest, and *$50* goes to the Principle of your Loan.

You slowly pay off your mortgage over a lengthy period of time while the bank acquires profit off your loan.

The Banks say it's ok because if you do the math of the 30-year loan, it adds up to *6%* per year on the principal balance of your loan and the very last month it reverses, you are paying *$950* in principal and *$50* in interest.

Does that sound like 6%?

The following diagram is an example of an Amortization Mortgage:

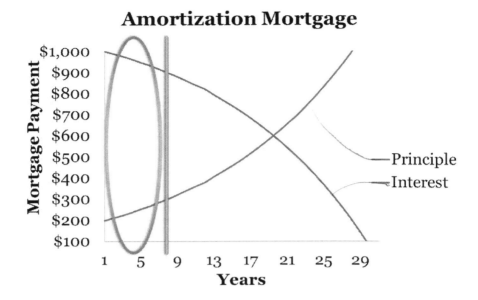

Figure 4: Amortization Mortgage

Five to seven years go by, and typically most people sell and move, or want a lower payment. The bank may start calling to suggest consolidation of your debt by refinancing your mortgage to get a lower rate and to pay off your credit cards.

Your Amortization starts over, and you are in a cycle of paying interest first and principal last. Many people do this repeatedly. Only a very few people ever complete the 30-years of their loan.

Mortgage Loans are the most expensive lending option in existence.

According to Wikipedia, The Truth in Lending Act (TILA) of 1968 is United States federal law designed to promote the informed use of consumer credit, by requiring disclosures about its terms and cost to standardize the way costs associated with borrowing are calculated and disclosed.

The Truth and Lending Statement that the government requires lenders to have you sign when you sign for your mortgage states that if you are paying the minimum payment every month for *30* years, you will pay **$431,676** total for a **$200,000** Mortgage.

30 Year Mortgage Loan at 6%

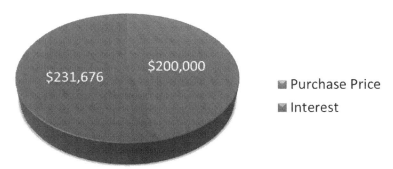

$231,676 $200,000

■ Purchase Price
■ Interest

Total Cost of Loan is $431,676.38

Figure 5: Cost of 30 Year Mortgage

Hmmm...that doesn't sound like **6%**. That is **120%** of the original amount you borrowed. Just generally of thumb that I like to use when looking at rates, take the original rate, double it and add a zero. That is converting it to simple interest, converting it to the same scale, like temperature degrees, Celsius to Fahrenheit.

The Average Person sees the **6%** and would rather pay the advertised **6%** when in all reality they are paying ***120%***. Thus, the more attractive number would be the ***21%*** line of credit or credit card.

The ***Wealthy Mindset*** pulls back the curtain and understands these scales. They see these Loans as being far more expensive than the *Lines of credit* at 21%.

The ***Employee Mindset*** thinks credit cards and *lines of credit* are bad, and that using them is not good. In reality, they can be a good thing to get out of debt.

The ***Employee Mindset*** uses Cash as currency. The ***Wealthy Mindset*** person uses leverage as currency. Cash is not currency cash is velocity, the reason is cash loses value over time.

The ***Wealthy Mindset*** does not keep a lot of cash. They keep a lower amount compared to the ratio of their net worth. Inflation is 3.5% a year that we are losing on the dollar. Money loses money if it just sits there under the mattress or in a checking account.

Employee Mindset ➡   Cash = Currency
Wealthy Mindset ➡ Leverage = Currency
                                        Cash = Velocity

How do you turn Money into an asset?

You move it; velocity is the asset of money. The liability of money is stagnation. Moving money around appropriately can turn money into an asset. Leverage is Currency.

Keeping money in your savings account is not keeping up with inflation.   You strategically use borrowed money to increase return on investment. That is **Leverage**.

For example; Donald Trump bought Trump Towers. He didn't work a 9-to-5 job and wrote a check out of his checking account to pay for it. He leveraged it. Now that's on a significant scale.

On the small scale if the **Employee Mindset** learned to leverage money and keep it moving they can save money and keep more wealth.

To leverage money, you need to keep it moving.

When you get your paycheck, you need to deploy quickly. If you keep it in a checking and savings account, your money is losing value. A savings account with a **0.2%** interest does not keep up with inflation. You need to move all your money to your Line of Credit or Credit Cards quickly. This is the point when someone tells me I sound crazy.

> # *Yes, every penny you make needs to be put on a line of credit or credit card.*

The beautiful thing about this is that you can use this 2-way lending from your credit card or line of credit to buy groceries, pay for gas, pay utilities, etc. You can't do that with a Mortgage. Mortgages are a one-way lending. You can't swipe your mortgage to buy groceries; you can't swipe your mortgage to buy gas.

Now you're thinking, well wait a minute. You can't pay your mortgage with a credit card. Yes, that is correct, but you can link my checking account to your credit card or line of credit as Overdraft.

If I don't have the funds in my checking account than they will just pull from my line of credit. I keep my checking account at zero because money loses money. I write a check for my mortgage it gets drawn from my line of credit.

There are a lot of benefits on doing it this way. Most **Lines of credit** require that you at least make a *$300* deposit on the account. Just to make sure you are going to pay back the Line of credit and get their interest. When you put your whole paycheck on that line of credit, for example, $3500 a month their minimum requirement is satisfied, and you don't even have to budget for it.

> ## Do not save. Savings is for chumps.

The banks use that savings just to lend right back to you. If you Leverage your money, you will never have to save.

The **Employee Mindset** is very competitive about how much they make. The **Wealthy Mindset** is collaborative and sees a deal in every conversation. The wealthy are focused on cash flow. If the cash flow is not enough the **Wealthy Mindset** are not interested in the deal.

THE THIRD PILLAR IS BUSINESS.

To incorporate the **Wealthy Mindset** means owning a business and operating that business profitably. You will never enjoy financial freedom while being an employee of a company. You must switch your mindset from the **Employee Mindset** to the **Wealthy Mindset.**

Entrepreneurs have an incredible opportunity to create something from nothing, in a way that's not possible working for someone else. The wealthy lifestyle is addicting and incorporates an astonishing amount of freedom.

THE FOURTH PILLAR IS REAL ESTATE.

There is leverage power in real estate. Therefore, I like real estate as an investment category. You can't leverage gold, but you can leverage real estate. With enough real estate I can play monopoly and charge people rent. I build my wealth by having real estate that has tenants and therefore rent and cash flow.

Want to play monopoly?

Also, the following are some examples of **Employee Mindset** that I have come across as I've been coaching people.

I was talking to a person the other day who works two jobs. They work four ten hour shifts and then go to a serving job at a restaurant. They talked about how much time they have left in each day, and it was about 30 minutes when all was said and done.

We accounted for getting ready for work, traveling to and from work, getting ready for bed, paying the bills, etc. After reviewing all the time, this person spent this person realized they only have about 30 minutes to an hour of free time in the day, which added up to around five hours total of extra time they had per week.

I asked, "What do you like to do with those five hours a week?" They said, "Well, let's go clubbing!" That's what they liked to do with their five extra hours each week.

This person dreams of becoming a musician and a famous performer, but it's hard to become a renowned performer by working 60 to 70 hours weeks and then going to the club with any left-over time. It doesn't work by magic. There must be time for songs writing, practicing, social media marketing, and a day job.

In this example, a mentality switch needs to happen. There needs to be a shift from an ***Employee Mindset*** – working two jobs and spending free time partying – to a ***Wealthy Mindset***.

We talked about the possibility of quitting the jobs and taking on one to two gigs a week to pay the bills. We ran the numbers together, and that's all this person would need to make up for the income received from both jobs. One to two gigs per week! That's a total of 6 hours versus 60 to 70 hours spent at a W-2 job.

The rest of the time could be spent on building the dream. AND – the 6 hours spent would be in music, furthering that business instead of working in an area in which they have no interest.

Another example of an ***Employee Mindset*** is paying rent versus paying a mortgage. Whether you pay, rent or have a mortgage for the home you live in you are making somebody else wealthy because you're either paying someone else's mortgage, or paying interest on your own mortgage.

A ***Wealthy Mindset*** would want to collect rent or collect a mortgage payment. Rentals are probably one of the primary property investments people think about when they think of investing in real estate, but many people don't know about holding financial notes. You can finance someone's mortgage for them, collect the interest, and collect the payments back as well.

In this example, the ***Employee Mindset*** is paying the rent or the mortgage, whereas, the ***Wealthy Mindset*** is collecting the rent or the mortgage.

Here is another related real-life example. I had a situation with one of the *Fix-N-Flips* I was managing where I had to fire a contractor who was delinquent in their performance on the property.

I called the City's Constable's Office and had the Constable come to the property. He was there to make sure everything ran smoothly while I fired this contractor and asked him to leave the property.

The contractor left, and while I was paying the Constable for his time, he mentioned he invests in real estate, and that is his retirement plan for him and his wife. He has been doing it for years and made so much money doing it that he has retirement accounts set up and funded for all of his living children and grandchildren.

The constable chooses to work because he loves being a constable and serving in that in that capacity. He had a ***Wealthy Mindset*** early on and invested his money in real estate. Not only is he able to live off the money he made from his investments, but he is able to create a future for himself, his children, and his grandchildren because of his ***Wealthy Mindset***.

TRADITIONAL EDUCATION TRAP

Getting an education and getting a degree are very different things. Many people mix those two concepts up, and they don't realize there is a difference.

The ***Employee Mindset*** is as follows: I've got to get that degree. It doesn't matter what I learned in the interim, it's the degree, it's the piece of paper I'm going to take to my future boss and say, and ask for a job? And you trade that degree for a job.

The ***Wealthy Mindset*** person does not think that way. Steve Jobs is a great example. He dropped out of Reed College because he couldn't afford it anymore, but he still dropped in on classes he wanted to gain knowledge from, like calligraphy.

You can watch Steve jobs give a commencement address at Stanford in 2005 on YouTube, but below is an excerpt from his speech:

"I never graduated from college. Truth be told, this is the closest I've ever gotten to a college graduation [...] I dropped out of Reed College after the first 6 months, but then stayed around as a drop-in for another 18 months or so before I really quit. So why did I drop out?

"It started before I was born. My biological mother was a young, unwed college graduate student, and she decided to put me up for adoption. She felt very strongly that I should be adopted by college graduates, so everything was all set for me to be adopted at birth by a lawyer and his wife. Except that when I popped out, they decided at the last minute that they really wanted a girl.

So, my parents, who were on a waiting list, got a call in the middle of the night asking: "We have an unexpected baby boy; do you want him?" They said: "Of course." My biological mother later found out that my mother had never graduated from college and that my father had never graduated from high school. She refused to sign the final adoption papers. She only relented a few months later when my parents promised that I would someday go to college.

"And 17 years later I did go to college. But I naively chose a college that was almost as expensive as Stanford, and all my working-class parents' savings were being spent on my college tuition. After six months, I couldn't see the value in it. I had no idea what I wanted to do with my life and no idea how college was going to help me figure it out.

And here I was spending all the money my parents had saved their entire life. So, I decided to drop out and trust that it would all work out okay. It was pretty scary at the time, but looking back it was one of the best decisions I ever made. The minute I dropped out I could stop taking the required classes that didn't interest me, and begin dropping in on the ones that looked interesting.

It wasn't all romantic. I didn't have a dorm room, so I slept on the floor in friends' rooms, I returned Coke bottles for the 5¢ deposits to buy food with, and I would walk the 7 miles across town every Sunday night to get one good meal a week at the Hare Krishna temple. I loved it. And much of what I stumbled into by following my curiosity and intuition turned out to be priceless later on. Let me give you one example:

Reed College at that time offered perhaps the best calligraphy instruction in the country. Throughout the campus, every poster, every label on every drawer, was beautifully hand calligraphed. Because I had dropped out and didn't have to take the normal classes, I decided to take a calligraphy class to learn how to do this. I learned about serif and sans-serif typefaces, about varying the amount of space between different letter combinations, about what makes great typography great. It was beautiful, historical, artistically subtle in a way that science can't capture, and I found it fascinating.

None of this had even a hope of any practical application in my life. But 10 years later, when we were designing the first Macintosh computer, it all came back to me. And we designed it all into the Mac. It was the first computer with beautiful typography. If I had never dropped in on that single course in college, the Mac would have never had multiple typefaces or proportionally spaced fonts. And since Windows just copied the Mac, it's likely that no personal computer would have them. If I had never dropped out, I would have never dropped in on this calligraphy class, and personal computers might not have the wonderful typography that they do. Of course, it was impossible to connect the dots looking forward when I was in college. But it was very, very clear looking backward 10 years later.

Again, you can't connect the dots looking forward; you can only connect them looking backward. So, you have to trust that the dots will somehow connect in your future. You have to trust in something — your gut, destiny, life, karma, whatever. This approach has never let me down, and it has made all the difference in my life." ~ Steve Jobs

Because he dropped in on the calligraphy class after he had dropped out, he learned how to draw calligraphy, that's one of the main reasons why we have fonts today on our computers and why we had fonts on the Macintosh in 1984 instead of just the plain text appearing on the screen.

Steve Jobs had a ***Wealthy Mindset*** from the very beginning. He valued education over the piece of paper that you get at the end. One of the points I want to make while we're talking about education is we are trained to be employees by being influenced to get a lower end degree. If that happens, you can expect to be an employee on the "***40, 40, 40***" track.

Now, I'm not telling you to drop out of college or not to go to college, quite the opposite, actually. ***GET EDUCATED***! It is the investment that will return the highest yield again and again in your life.

> ***Education and knowledge are the most important things you can strive for.***

I am only trying to put into perspective the failings of society in education. People tend to pay to get the degree, not the education; that's the ***Employee Mindset***! Once you start to realize that it's not about the degree, it opens so many more opportunities for you in your education process.

If you get a bachelor's degree, you can expect to be an employee making a decent salary at a decent job, meaning: middle-class, maybe lower in management. Possibly if you get a higher education degree, a master's degree, you'll land a job in middle management, corporate, make a cool $100,000 - $300,000 a year, excellent. Doctors make a little bit more. Maybe you can start a practice of your own if you're in medicine or whatever the case might be.

The main problem, again, is with that **Employee Mindset**. You will only make money if you are at work, which means you're still in that same trap of trading your time for money. Whether you're a doctor or an orthodontist, if you are not in your office practicing on patients you're not getting paid. So, while they may be rich, unless they are doing other things behind the scenes, they're not necessarily wealthy.

The education system that's in place teaches you to be an employee and educates you to be in the **Employee Mindset**. It's hard to change that mindset, especially if you have gone through years of formal education.

Of those I coach, I find that the more difficult clients I help educate are the ones with a more traditional education. It takes work to change a mindset that has been ingrained through years and years of traditional education, especially if they have higher education. We've got to change some of those practices.

One of the things I've noticed about success is that in school they teach a few ideas that I find can hold people back from real progress. They teach you that copying is not allowed. If you copy off someone else's homework, if you copy off someone else's test you're punished for that; in real life, copying is called success.

Think back to my story that I told at the beginning of this book. The way that I started down the path towards success was by finding out what other people were doing and by mimicking it. A lot of people find wealth that way, and it is not a huge secret. It's not like the wealthy have gotten together and are trying to hide anything from anybody. It is a simple formula.

The wealthy own businesses and invest in real estate, and if you want to be wealthy, you copy the people that are doing that. Another thing I find interesting is taught in public schools. The education system teaches that failure is something that holds you back, you don't get to progress through failure, you get held back, and you must do it again. Failure is something looked down upon and something to be ashamed of.

> *In life, failure often creates the biggest learning experiences.*

My father-in-law often says, "Nobody successes their way to success. They fail their way to success." One of my mentors, a very wealthy person, whom I have a lot of respect for, told me once, "I'm successful because I'm standing on a mountain of my failures."

What I get from that is he didn't look at failure as something that was going to hold him back or push him down. He looked at failure as a learning experience. Instead of failures being obstacles that knock us down and hold us there, we can rearrange them and build a structure that we can stand on to get to the next step.

CASH FLOW

One thing the **Wealthy Mindset** focus on much more than employees is cash flow. Employees have a job, they receive income from that job, and they usually have expenses that equal their incomes with maybe a little bit left over – basically living paycheck to paycheck – while the wealthy focus on cash flow.

As I've said multiple times already, the wealthy build businesses and invest in real estate. Those are tangible things that create cash flow, and cash flow is something you'll receive regardless of whether you're working or not. If you don't show up for work because you're in Europe with the family, your business, if you built it right, is making you money even while you're away.

Rent is a primary form of cash flow for a lot of investors. For those in the ***Employee Mindset***, that rent check is the most important thing each month – "I have to go to work because I have to pay the rent." Rent is, for some, that magic check that must get written every month. "We can't go to Disneyland this year, sorry. I've got to go to work so I can pay the rent." We can't do this, we can't do that." "I can't throw you a big birthday party because - sorry, I don't have enough money, I've got to pay the rent."

That rent check is the magic check people always write because that's everybody's most important check of the month, and rightfully so - you must have a place to live. The wealthy have figured out that it's more desirable to be on the other side of that check; then they can be the ones going to Disneyland or throwing the big birthday party.

Cash flow is something that allows you to pull yourself out of the actual work and continue to make money. Those in the ***Employee Mindset*** are always focused on what they make. "I make $3,500 per month." "I make $100,000 per year." "I make $50 per hour." This is a telltale sign of someone in the ***Employee Mindset***. They will tell you how much money they make.

What they don't tell you is how much they spend every month. I would bet that it is close to that same number. That is why the wealthy don't focus on what they make; they focus on their monthly cash flow. Cash flow can be expressed by a simple equation:

$$\textbf{\textit{Cash flow = Income – Expenses}}$$

If you are spending every dollar you bring in every month, your cash flow is ***zero***. A ***Wealthy Mindset*** person will be completely disinterested in that model regardless of how much you make.

You could make one billion dollars per week, but if you are spending that much, then your cash flow is still zero. Your cash flow is a significant indicator: it will tell you if you are on the right track or if you need to buy more assets and stop buying liabilities.

The ***Wealthy Mindset*** spends their money on investments that will *make* them more money. Those with the ***Employee Mindset*** spend their money on things that will only *cost* them money.

Robert Kiyosaki, the author of *Rich Dad, Poor Dad*, is one of my favorite authors. He calls the things that cost money and don't make money "*doodads.*" He does a fantastic job of explaining the difference between an asset and a liability and how the things he calls doodads (TVs, boats, vacations) don't make you any money. If you haven't read his bestseller *Rich Dad, Poor Dad* you must! He does a phenomenal job of contrasting the **Employee Mindset** and the **Wealthy Mindset**.

At the end of the day, the people in the **Employee Mindset** spend that little bit of extra money they have, those few hundred dollars, to buy a TV rather than buying stock. The **Employee Mindset** pays a boat payment rather than purchasing a bank note which could be yielding interest, and when I say bank note, I don't mean a CD. (A banknote is directly funding someone's loan, and receiving the payments.)

> **Instead of buying "doodads," invest your money in something that will make you more money.**

I want to do a short exercise here. Think of something you want that you'd pay $20,000 for if you had it, whether you have the cash or whether you had $20,000 on a credit card or loan.

If I asked you to use that money to invest $20,000 in real estate right now, would you hesitate? Maybe you had a car in mind or a vacation.

When you think about taking that same cash and buying a little house to rent out – well, that's when you started to get knots in your stomach, right? We've been programmed by society to think like employees, and again I want to clarify that it's okay to think that way,

I would estimate that **95%** of people are in the **Employee Mindset**, even sports stars are employees. I'm sure they are living their dreams, making a lot of money, and probably happy, but they are still employees.

Society needs people with an **Employee Mindset**. If everybody started doing what I'm talking about here, society would kind of collapse because there wouldn't be any consumers.

I am talking about becoming a creator, creating products, housing, jobs, whatever it may be that people consume, and getting paid for it.

When presented with purchasing a big item or purchasing an investment, like real estate, employees are of the mindset, "What is that going to cost me?" In most cases, the investment costs much more than the TV or the boat and doesn't yield the same immediate emotional fix that those other investments do.

Usually, the employee passes on the investment because it costs too much and doesn't fulfill an emotional need. The wealthy have changed their mindset and ask a different question: "How much money is that going to make me?"

I know many **Wealthy Mindset** people who don't own expensive cars. When I asked one of my mentors why he bought a 2005 truck instead of a new 2016 truck, his answer was, "It's not going to make me anything, it gets me from point A to point B. I spend my money on things that are going to provide a return for me."

This example drives the idea (no pun intended) of spending our first dollar (the money we make from our job or business) on an asset (something that will make more money), then spend the money the asset has made for us (the second dollar) on things we need to live. By thinking this way and structuring your life around that idea, you will never run out of money.

DRIVE

Drive is something that separates the successful from the unsuccessful. Everybody has dreams. Everybody once had a dream of being a fireman, a policeman, a musician, an actor, a superhero, and so on, when they were young, but not everyone has the drive to become their dream.

My dream, when I was young, was to own businesses. I wanted to be the guy that ran the company; I'm living that dream right now, and it's fantastic.

> ***The dream is the seed, and it instills in us the desire to get to a destination, the drive is what gets us to that destination.***

If you were to do a survey, I would imagine that more people are not living their dreams versus people you do. Many people have justified their dreams away because they feel they need to make money now, so they end up settling and staying in one or more jobs that are not related to their real dream.

Those who are living their dream made sacrifices along the way, and they wanted to make the right sacrifices that would lead to their dream. What is going to connect people to the dream that they originally had is drive. Regardless of where we are, if we're three steps away from our dream or 300 steps away, we have a journey to take, and it's going to take some work to get there.

The work is not going to be easy. It's going to be rough, and hard choices will have to be made, such as in the earlier example of partying versus learning how to become successful a musician.

If you're not willing to spend the time, and not ready to make the sacrifices to get to that dream, then you have a lack of drive. **Drive** is the thing that's going to push you to accomplish the things you want to achieve. You will need to get things done, and there will be no excuses.

The first thing that you need to understand about drive is that you must be educated on what it's going to take to accomplish your dream.

> *Education/knowledge is the most significant key to accomplishing anything great.*

You must know what you're up against. You must understand what needs to be accomplished to reach your goal.

Again, we're not talking about getting a degree. The knowledge you will need to be wealthy requires real, applicable education, not just a degree.

Real estate investing requires education. You can't just go out and do it, or you're going to lose money. You need to be educated on how to do it correctly by someone who has done it before. Your education is going to lay out specific steps and tasks you need to take on a regular basis to accomplish your goal.

Drive has certain requirements which yield certain rewards. Drive really is the vehicle that leads you from wherever you are in life right now (whether you're just starting out or whether you're almost there) to your dream.

There are three requirements to maintain drive: obedience, sacrifice, and mission.

Figure 6: Maintain Drive

The first requirement is obedience.

When you're educated on what it is you want to do you understand the roadmap, and if you're obedient to that roadmap you receive the reward for your obedience: faith in yourself.

As you continue to follow what is required of you to get to your dream, you have renewed faith in yourself to be able to accomplish your dream. Your excitement is renewed on a regular basis.

One thing that I have seen push people away from accomplishing their dream is that they get discouraged. They allow negative thoughts to creep into their mind, *"I can't do this"*, *"I just don't have it in me"*, *"I need to get a second job"*, and *"All my friends are saying that I should just give this pushes people to recoil and to disengage."*

If you focus on accomplishing the things you want to achieve, and you are obedient to the things that you learn, you will renew your excitement about your goals repeatedly.

Habitual positive thinking and focus are the way to shift your mindset from an **Employee Mindset** to a **Wealthy Mindset**. You will also develop a sense of urgency to complete your goals. They seem realistic and attainable.

The next requirement of the drive is sacrifice.

The reward of sacrifice is that sacrifice yields hope. For example, you may be interested in attending a workshop to learn how to invest in real estate; however, there may be a $5,000 workshop fee. That workshop fee may seem like a big sacrifice.

Maybe, to pay for the workshop, you forego a vacation this year. That's a real sacrifice.

But what does sacrifice provide for you?

If you want to be a real estate investor, the workshop, which you have sacrificed for, is going to provide you with the needed knowledge. That knowledge is the hope you need to accomplish your dream.

Before your sacrifice, you had no hope of becoming an investor because you had no idea how to invest. Now, because of your sacrifice, you have that knowledge, which gives you that hope.

The last requirement of drive is having a mission, and the reward for having a mission is charity.

Every successful business has a mission statement. They have a clear reason why they're doing what they are doing. The poorly thought-out mission statements focus on money, and a successful business is not always about money.

I have found that sometimes you can have enough money, so money isn't always a motivation. Even if you don't have the ideal amount of money, it doesn't always motivate the way you think it will. So, having a mission, having an apparent reason you're doing what you want to do, is the way to motivate yourself beyond money.

Maybe part of your mission is about improving the living conditions of others, or making education more accessible and affordable, or investing in healthcare technology.

Whatever your mission is, it's going to lead to a greater sense of helping others and making the world a better place. I've learned through being a businessman that karma, or whatever you want to call it, is real.

As you start building your business and making decisions, good or bad, they come back to you in the business community. You begin to build off relationships, and people start to see that you're not just a greedy business person; you are good and caring. That's what people tend to gravitate toward.

> ***People are more willing to give you their money when they feel like they can trust you.***

Living a life of abundance and giving will come back to you. Giving before gaining is a philosophy that will also return to you. Your choices tend to come back to you. As you are transformed into a more charitable business person, success will be returned to you.

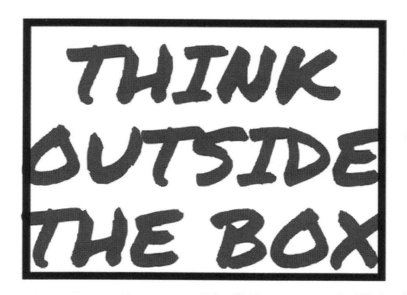

Figure 7: Think Outside the Box

Thinking outside the box is more than just a cliché. You must approach life with a fresh new way of looking at ways to generate income. You must switch your **Employee Mindset** to a **Wealthy Mindset**. Conceptualize the life you want to lead and imagine abundance.

RICH VERSUS WEALTHY

We've touched on being rich versus being wealthy a little bit, but I want to dive into it more right now. One of the essential things to understand is the difference between rich and wealthy. You can have a lot of money, and you can make a lot of money.

Your paycheck could be seven figures a month, and yet, you can still be an employee and still have an **Employee Mindset**. Just because you make a lot of money doesn't mean you are wealthy; it means you're rich, and many wealthy people lose their money.

There are a lot of examples of celebrities that have had a lot of money and lost it all. If you're not adequately educated on how to turn your money into actual wealth, it can be gone quickly. Having principles in place and understanding how to build wealth and keep it is going to turn your money into true wealth.

Money is an advantage, so if you make a lot of money at your job, you've got an advantage over other people, but that doesn't necessarily mean you're always going to have it. If today, you could stop doing the work you do every day that's supposed to generate money; if you can move forward from that scenario and have enough money coming in to cover all your expenses: you're wealthy.

That's that point of which, according to the author Robert Kiyosaki, you're out of the rat race – you no longer must go to your job, even if it's a job you created.

Once you have enough money coming in from passive investments you can decide, "I'm not going to do anything for a year," and money still comes in and pays the bills – that's when you're wealthy.

> ## *If you want to create wealth, you need to accept that wealth isn't a bad thing.*

A lot of people think wealthy people are evil. For some reason, people think their bosses are greedy, or the owner of the company they work for is greedy and only wants money. You'll need to get over that mindset if you want to be wealthy.

Wealthy people do a lot for society. The very fact that you're working for a wealthy person shows you a lot of things about them, one of which is that that wealthy person created your job. Another ***Wealthy Mindset*** person most likely created your living space.

Wealthy people create and own businesses that create jobs and invest in real estate that house people. The reason some people in society dislike the rich is that they think wealthy people pay less in taxes. Well, they do. The tax code is an incentive program, not a penalty.

If wealthy people don't create jobs, the government must take on that responsibility, and they don't want to; they are not set up for it, so they rely on the wealthy to create jobs. How do they reward people who are doing that? They give them tax incentives.

If wealthy people don't create housing, who will create housing?

The government will. What does the government do to encourage people to create housing? They give better tax rates and tax incentives to those who do.

That is why people who own businesses and invest in real estate pay a lower percentage in taxes than people who are consumers. People who consume these jobs and consume the housing are consumers and have the ***Employee Mindset***. And consumers get taxed while ***Wealthy Mindset*** creators get tax breaks.

So, if you want to be wealthy, you've got to accept that things like tax incentives are not a bad thing. Money is an inanimate object; it can't be good or bad. It is what the people who have the money do with it that is good or bad.

RISK

There are a lot of things that hold people back, and a big one is risk. It's risky to start your own business, right? We've been taught that there's nothing as secure as having a job.

Nothing is as secure as going to school, getting a degree, and getting a job. Because that is the idea of being financially secure, there's a fear of risk that's been created in us.

Well, I've got news for a lot of people: when you have a job, it can only take one person to say, "***you're fired***," and that's not real security.

> ### *A large source of income for me is a business I own.*

It has over 200 clients and creates cash flow. For me to lose that cash flow or be fired, I would have to have 200 people all decide on the same day that they don't want to do business with my company anymore. That is real financial security because the likelihood of that happening is very, very low.

> ## *Risk management is knowledge about your fear and overcoming it.*

A good example of this concept can be seen in a story about my wife. My wife fears spiders. Eventually, we'll get her to overcome that fear, but I've told her repeatedly, the one thing that will make you overcome your fear of spiders is knowledge. If she would study spiders and understand them, understand why they do what they do, and the biology behind them, that's going to change her fear.

It's the same with investing, and it's the same with building a business. If you have a fear of investing then get educated. Knowledge is exactly the thing that's going to erase that fear.

SHORT-TERM VS LONG-TERM FEARS

We'll dive into knowledge versus fear a little bit more, but let's talk about fear. *Fear* is defined in Webster's dictionary as, "***an unpleasant, sometimes strong emotion caused by an anticipation or awareness of danger***" or "**anxious concern.**" I break it down even further and compare with the terms ***short-term fear*** and ***long-term fear***.

Long-term fear can be a good thing. Long-term fears are things like, "If I keep doing what I'm doing, I'll end up staying in this dead-end job forever, I'm never going to reach my dreams." That's a *long-term fear*.

Long-term fear is often (though it needs to be checked) something to embrace. However, *short-term fear* a lot of times is the exact opposite of *long-term fear*.

Short-term fear is the most dangerous fear because **short-term fear** can overshadow that **long-term fear**. **Short-term fear** will show up something like this, "I can't quit my job now because I have a car payment and rent due this month."

See how they are opposite?

For most people, the *short-term fear* is a much louder voice. Most people cower to their *short-term fear*s and are unwilling to take a risk. Taking that risk could be the difference in money for retirement and the ability to buy your time to do fun things you have wanted to do for a long time.

If you are regularly checking your fears against each other, you can usually tell which fear is just an excuse and which fear simply needs to be overcome – and it can be overcome with knowledge.

Figure 8: Believe in Yourself

Some of the fears that I often hear when I'm talking to people about learning how to invest in real estate, building a business, or building wealth? One of them is, "I don't have the money to invest."

> *I invested in my first real estate property without using any of my own money.*

I didn't have any money so I couldn't use my own, but I was able to do it using other people's money because of what I learned from an education course I took. With that knowledge, I raised enough money to buy real estate.

Another fear I often hear from people is they don't have the experience needed. Again, that fear of lack of experience can be replaced by knowledge. If I were to sit down with you and explain exactly how to do a remodel on a home to resell it for a profit, and we crunch the numbers together, you'd feel a lot more comfortable than just going into it blind.

> ### *Knowledge can make the fear of no experience disappear.*

You can leverage another people's knowledge as well. Often times I've found it's the people in my life and the networks I build through various things I do, whether it's business or real estate, through which I find someone who can help me solve a problem. If I don't know something, then those people can be brought in, and they can help me fix the issue.

> ### *Faith is knowledge.*

We talked a little bit about having faith in yourself and just obeying the steps that you learn as you begin to develop the skills necessary for reaching your dream. Whether your dream is being a famous musician or being the best firefighter or investing in real estate, as you go through and learn the steps required to reach your dream, and you're obedient to those steps, you're going to develop faith in yourself.

Sometimes all it takes is to show up. I would agree with whoever said that **90%** of success is simply showing up. Just by going to the class, by learning, by showing up to your coaching appointment and getting that coaching, you're gaining knowledge.

As you start to implement that knowledge, you gain renewed faith in yourself and are able to do those things you want to do.

I think the fear of failure is the most significant fear people have. There is even a scientific name for it, *Atychiphobia.* We briefly discuss how we are taught that failure is a bad thing. It's not true.

> *Failure is not a bad thing; failure is an essential step in the learning process.*

I've started companies; in fact, I've probably started close to 30 companies, I haven't counted recently, but most of them have failed.

Only a handful of those companies are still around and provide a source of income for my family and me. But every time one fails, I learn something – and the next one is that much stronger.

Remember what my mentor said, we stand on a mountain of our failures with a few successes that make us wealthy and build our wealth. It's built upon a foundation of mistakes and ways we learned not to do something.

What if Edison had given up after one attempt at building a light bulb?

How would the last 100 years have been different for all of humanity? Don't hold back, you have nothing to be ashamed of, and you don't need permission from anybody to be successful.

Chapter 2

Wealthy People Own Businesses

Figure 9: Success

The *second* key to **Mindset to Millionaire** is to *own a business*. Wealthy people own one or more businesses. The differences between how business owners and employees are different are how they handle their money.

It is important to understand that **Wealthy Mindset** people own a business for many reasons, one being that a business protects you as an individual from liability more than just being an employee. In the eyes of the law, a company has a separate identity from the owners.

Nelson Rockefeller, the grandson of John D Rockefeller, said, "***The secret to success is to own nothing, but control everything***." ("Nelson Rockefeller." BrainyQuote.com.)

> ## *You don't want anything in your personal name.*

Let me illustrate this using a hypothetical situation. Let's say you are driving your car and drop your phone between the seats. You reach down to grab it and when you look up an old lady is crossing the road, and you hit her. Even if she doesn't die and is only injured, she can still sue you for basically everything you own.

When you own your house, car, have savings, or investments; everything you have is available for the court to award to that person as restitution for an incident. From a liability standpoint, the wealthy own a business to protect themselves.

Part of keeping that wealth is protecting it – you must put a big fence around your fat cows.

> **Being wealthy is not just accumulating wealth which is money and assets, but it is keeping that wealth.**

Liability protection is something huge for business owners, and employees don't get to take advantage of it. Most don't even understand the benefit. Let's look at the above scenario from the perspective of someone who has structured their lives and their assets appropriately.

In this hypothetical scenario, you own a construction business that makes a lot of money. You need several vehicles and tools for your line of business, so you start another business that owns all those assets and leases them to your construction company. You have your personal residence, vehicles, and your retirement accounts in a living revocable trust. All your assets are separated and protected by different entities.

Now, let's say that same scenario happens but with a work truck. Your work truck is in your equipment entity mentioned above. The beautiful thing about having the separate entities is the only things that can be available to the courts to award to this person for restitution are the things inside that entity.

Your house, personal car, and other personal assets are protected, as well as, all your savings accounts and investments because they are not owned by the same entity as the vehicle in question.

Frequent travelers or people who live in big cities learn to keep their money in different pockets. When I lived in Madrid, Spain I would put a little bit of money in each pocket so if I was pickpocketed (which happened a lot on the subway) they only got the money that was in one pocket, but they not all of it.

> *The wealthy put their money and assets in different "pockets." by structuring with entities.*

If you have a small amount of money or assets, you will need fewer pockets. As your wealth starts to grow, you protect it by creating more and more pockets.

Figure 10: Own a Business

The other big reason the wealthy own their own business is for tax purposes. As an employee you get a total of 15 tax write-offs; there are over 300 for businesses.

The IRS wants to know what your Adjusted Gross Income (AGI) is, and that's what you pay taxes on. If your AGI is ***$40,000***, then you pay taxes on ***$40,000***. The goal is for you to be able to use as many write-offs as legally, morally, and ethically possible to offset your AGI.

If you have $100 in write-offs, and you made $40,000 from your business, your $100 in write-offs is subtracted from that forty thousand. So now you have $39,900 which becomes your new AGI, and you pay taxes on $39,900 rather than $40,000.

If you get educated on how to do this, it can lead to quite the savings on your taxes every year. With 300 plus write-offs available to adjust your AGI, you could end up lowering your tax liability substantially.

I want to do a quick illustration. Let's say as an employee you gross $100,000. For employees, the government utilizes W-2s, which means the government already has an agreement with your employer that they get your money before you do. The government will take roughly 30% of your $100,000 leaving you with $70,000 before your employer even writes your check.

I find it humorous that people in the ***Employee Mindset*** view this as a convenience when really Uncle Sam has his hands in your pocket. The people in the ***Wealthy Mindset*** view this as something to avoid. Now, let's say that your expenses throughout the rest of the year are $70,000. At the end of the year, you end up with $0.

If you were to make the same $100,000 annual gross income as a business, you would not be subject to W-2 withholdings, so the government isn't taking their money first – they take their money last. You get to write off all your expenses first.

Let's use the same number here and say that all your expenses are $70,000. As a business owner, you get to put most of that above-the-line on your Adjusted Gross Income (AGI), you get to subtract the $70,000 from the $100,000. So instead of your AGI is $100,000, your AGI is now $30,000 because you take out your expenses first. Now you're paying taxes on $30,000 and only paying $10,000 in taxes.

You have $20,000 left over, so you made money simply by owning a business.

> ***You did nothing different on the numbers you brought in; you just changed your mindset and saved money.***

Now you can reinvest that $20,000 in your business, you can hire new people and create new jobs which are what the government wants you to do.

Figure 11: Start your Business

The government wants you to provide jobs for people, which is why they give you those incentives so you can continue to create. You can invest in real estate or other investment options that will grow your wealth. It is easy to see why the wealthy prefer to own businesses rather than be employees.

Keep in mind that when you are creating your strategy, the law is particular about what you can and cannot take as a deduction. Always consult a Certified Public Accountant (CPA) when designing and implementing your tax strategy. Most importantly, never venture beyond that which is legal, moral, or ethical.

TIME

The time you spend as an employee at a job is building someone else's wealth. You're investing your time and trading it for money. You're able to support yourself, but the time you're investing is growing someone else's business, which is making **them** wealthy, **not you**.

> *Time is your most asset and your most sacred commodity.*

Many of the larger businesses and corporations have employees sign an intellectual property waiver during the hiring process. The waiver basically says that anything the employee invents or creates while in their employ is the property of the company.

If you work for a big tech company and you come up with a great idea for an app while on the job, guess who gets the first claim to the app? Not you. The tech company does. When you work for yourself, you are investing your time into building your own business. Any ideas you come up with are your property.

A word of caution: people tend to focus a lot of time on the operations side of their business as they start it. They buy a desk, a computer, put up a website, build their product and that's the extent of it. Then they wait. They think, "If you build it they will come," and sadly, that's just not the case. My dad aptly calls this "**Playing Office**." You've only done half of what is required to run a successful business.

There's a 50-50 rule when it comes to creating a business. There are two sides to your business, and they must be balanced. However, much time and resource you put into the operations and setup of your business, you must put an equal amount into the sales and marketing side.

You can make money with anything if you know how to sell, market, and advertise. The product is interchangeable. Look around you wherever you are at right now. Anything and everything you see was purchased at some point – at least once.

The art of marketing and selling are creating a transaction, and it's the transaction that makes you money. It's not building the business so that you can you can play office. It's building the business, so you can create transactions and trade your services or products for money to continue to build your business and wealth.

Remember as you are building your business after you have your great idea and get set up, it is imperative that you put just as much effort into marketing your business as you do the operations.

TIME MANAGEMENT

One of the most important things about building a business is managing your time. As you start to do this, you will be able to focus on the things that are really going to build your business. The wealthy understand that time is the only resource that you can't get more of, so they are comfortable trading their money for time.

Tasks such as mowing your lawn, cleaning your house, doing your taxes, or managing your accounts or bookkeeping are all very, very important and need to be done, but they don't necessarily need to be done by you.

You can spend your time with your family or reinvest it into the business. Those are things that don't need your specific attention unless you really are the best person for that job. Do what you're best at in your business, whether that be bookkeeping, operations, sales, or something else, and hire other people to do the rest.

My dad, who was the first millionaire I knew, always said that surrounding himself with competent professionals such as lawyers, accountants, bookkeepers, insurance agents, etc. helped him to become and stay successful.

Hire out things that can be done by people who are much better than you are at those tasks, and in the long run, it will cost you less money and time to hire someone more proficient.

It's important to understand that when I say that the wealthy run their own businesses – these aren't businesses that require their presence. The wealthy build businesses that they can step out of and still earn money. This model can apply to any business.

You may want to be an orthodontist, but you may also not want to have to be there. You can build an orthodontist practice that doesn't rely on you. Bring on other orthodontists and pay them well to do what they do best, and you can make money off them.

I wouldn't recommend creating a business that requires your constant presence to survive. Instead, create a system that you can step out of that will continue to run like a well-oiled machine.

There are ways to structure businesses and business operations that allow you to step eventually out of business and move on to something else.

> ### The ultimate goal is to have a business that you step out of and will continue to make money.

For the last four years, I have acted as CEO and head of Sales and Marketing for an SEO and Web Marketing firm I started with two partners. It got to a point where it paid us very well to be at the head of the business, but it also required a lot of time.

Because we built it right, with the intention of eventually stepping out of it, my partners and I were recently able to step down as CEO, COO, and CFO of the company and it continues to run and make money. It pays me every month without fail and requires little to no time on my part.

There is a great American example of the business model I am talking about. Ray Kroc didn't start McDonald's, but he had a hamburger at the McDonald's brothers' hamburger stand in San Bernardino, California.

Ray approached them and said something to the effect of, *"Hey, you have a fantastic family hamburger joint here. I'd be very interested in purchasing the franchising rights from you and building a few other locations."*

Of course, Ray Kroc knew what he had in mind. I don't know if he let them know what he had in mind, but he turned that somewhat successful hamburger stands into the international fast-food sensation, McDonald's.

We are reminded every time we pass a McDonald's sign that they have served billions and billions of hamburgers. The interesting thing is how many hamburgers do you think Ray Kroc flipped? My guess is zero. That's a testament to his ability to create a business he was able to step out of and continue to make money.

If you think about it, who is it that runs the local McDonald's chains? It's mostly teenagers working there. It's the most successful hamburger chain in the world, and it is run by *teenagers*! More to the point, is it the tastiest hamburger you've ever had? I'd guess that for most the answer is no. Yet, they are still the most successful. Why?

Ray Kroc created a system, and McDonald's operates by that system, where he didn't have to be at every single McDonald's flipping the burgers and managing the employees.

He created handbooks that set protocols on everything – from how you greet a customer to how you flip a hamburger. He outlined how managers manage the employees, how janitors were to clean, and how to replace the ice in the soda machines. He is able to this day, to duplicate these protocols and hand out copies wherever he built a McDonald's.

In 1974, Ray Kroc, the founder of McDonald's, was asked to speak to the MBA class at the University of Texas at Austin. A dear friend of mine, Keith Cunningham, was a student in that MBA class. After a powerful and inspiring talk, the class adjourned, and the students asked Ray if he would join them at their favorite hangout to have a few beers. Ray graciously accepted.

> *"What business am I in?" Ray asked once the group all had their beers in hand. No one answered, so Ray asked the question again. "What business do you think I am in?"*
>
> *The students laughed again, and finally one brave soul yelled out, "Ray, who in the world does not know that you're in the hamburger business."*
>
> *Ray chuckled. "That is what I thought you would say." He paused and then quickly said, "Ladies and gentlemen, I'm not in the hamburger business. My business is real estate."*
>
> *Keith said that Ray spent a good amount of time explaining his viewpoint. In their business plan, Ray knew that the primary business focus was*

to sell hamburger franchises, but what he never lost sight of was the location of each franchise. He knew that the real estate and its location was the most significant factor in the success of each franchise. Basically, the person that bought the franchise was also paying for buying the land under the franchise for Ray Kroc's organization.

McDonald's today is the largest single owner of real estate in the world, owning even more than the Catholic Church. Today McDonald's owns some of the most valuable intersections and street corners in America as well as in other parts of the world.

(Robert Kiyosaki, Sharon L. Lechter, Rich dad Poor dad, Hachette Book G, 2009)

Every McDonald's location sits on real estate that Ray's company owns. McDonald's are owned and operated by franchisees, not by corporate. McDonald's buys the land, leases the building back to the operator, and then charges franchise owner money to use the McDonald's name while they run the business.

It's genius. It is simultaneously running a business and investing in real estate. McDonald's is a prime example of the ideal business model that I am talking about – *a business that literally makes you money while you sleep*.

It is the Wealthy Mindset.

Chapter 3

Wealthy People Invest

The *third* key to **Mindset to Millionaire** is *investing*. I am going to illustrate and outline this point with an allegorical story. Then we will discuss applicable skills on how you can realistically start investing.

Figure 12: Time to Invest

THE HUNTER AND THE FARMER

There is a story of a hunter whose father had been a hunter. His grandfather had also been a hunter. Hunting was all his family had known for generations. His father took him out on his first hunt at a very young age and taught him the skills of the hunt.

His father taught him how to track his prey and how to conceal his scent. He also taught him to attract his prey, so it would be an easy kill.

One day he the father explained to him the importance of the hunt. "***Your village and your family rely on the hunt,***" he explained. "***One day it will fall on you to bring home food. If you fail, your village will go hungry, and your family will starve.***"

The young boy grew to appreciate and respect the reverence his father had for the hunt. He noticed his father never missed a day. Rain or shine, in sickness or health – even at the brink of death, his father would leave with bow and spear, his son at his side, to provide for those in his keep. As the young boy matured, his father leaned on him more and more to lead the hunt until one day it was his responsibility alone.

The boy, now a man, gave his all to the job. It was ingrained in him from a very young age that if he didn't get up in the morning and engage in the hunt, his family would suffer.

He looked forward to the day when he had a son of his own, and he thought how he would pass the lessons his father taught him on to his son.

The Hunter labored diligently to provide for his family, but one day he tracked a deer into a part of the wilderness that he was unfamiliar with. While running, some movement behind him distracted him, and he tripped over a root and fell and hit his head.

He was found days later by a member of his village and taken back to his camp. Though he survived the accident, he was not able to hunt for many months. His older parents and many members of his village, who relied on his efforts for food, went hungry.

At about the same time, in a valley not too far from where the hunter lived, there was a farmer. He toiled in his field, hoeing rows, and planting the seed. He started with a small patch of land, and he farmed it diligently.

He used what little money he had to buy seed for his first crops. He watered and tended his crop meticulously. He studied and learned how to better himself as a farmer and was very careful with his first yield.

After the first harvest, he set aside a certain percentage of his crop to plant for the next year's crop and expanded his farm. Every year he would allocate a certain percentage of his crop for the growth of the farm, so every year it would grow. It got to a point where he produced so much that he had a surplus. Merchants would come from far away to trade with him, and he and his family lived very well.

Figure 13: Farmer Allocation

The farmer produced so much from his farm that he had to hire farm hands to plant, tend, and harvest his crops for him. His crops and his stockpiles produced enough to feed his family for years, and the farm became self-sustaining; so much so that when the farmer grew old, retired, and eventually passed away, his family was taken care of for many years.

The parable of the Hunter and the Farmer illustrates the different mindsets we talked about in **Chapter 1**. If you have an **Employee Mindset**, you are a **hunter**. You must get up every day and go to work. You are paid for your time, but it only lasts a short while, and then you must go back and do it again.

Even if you are a good hunter, and you make a lot of money at your job, it will eventually run out, and you'll have to go back out and hunt some more.

Farmers have a different mentality. They understand that their crops are a renewable resource and that they will continue to yield and grow upon themselves. Hunters trade time for food. Farmers trade food for food.

> *Employees trade time for money and investors trade money for money.*

Farmers also could be more generous. Good farmers, who are educated and good at what they do usually have a surplus, which means plenty to share.

Hunters, by nature, live in more of a state of scarcity. They tend to be greedier. Not out of malice or because they are bad people, rather out of necessity. One kill will only last for a day or a few days at most. They must make sure their families are taken care of before they share.

Those in the **Employee Mindset** tend to live similar lives. Most of them live paycheck to paycheck, so there's not much left over to share – be it money or time.

Those in the **Wealthy Mindset** value their time more than money, so they use their money (not their time) to make more money. They usually end up with a surplus of both and are able to give of both.

There are many examples of this: Bill Gates, Warren Buffet, Elon Musk, and many others that may not be as visible. These individuals have made their fortunes and now focus their time and resources on making humanity better.

INVESTMENT AREAS

There are three major investment areas, namely, **business**, **real estate**, and **commodities**. There are also several ways to invest in these different areas. For simplicity, we will use gold as the investment.

1. You can buy the actual physical asset. For example, there are some people who invest in gold by purchasing it and storing it in their house.

2. You can invest in the "**option**" to buy an asset, which gives you the contractual right to purchase an asset at a set price on or by a set day. An example, in this case, is when you pay a fee to have the first right of refusal to purchase the gold in question at a set price on a set day. This gives you the freedom to buy the gold at the agreed on a price if it's higher on the day you must exercise the option. You would also have the option not to buy, but

you lose the "option fee" you paid to create the option in the first place.

Figure 14: Golden Egg

3. The third way to invest is by purchasing the "***paper***" version of gold, such as stocks bonds, or mutual funds. You are purchasing a paper certificate that says you own a certain amount of gold in a company. If you buy "***paper***" gold, it means the gold is yours, but it is stored somewhere. The nice thing about investing in paper is you can dice up the percentages of the asset, or gold, to be affordable to the masses.

It is interesting to note that the dollar bill used to be a paper note for gold. Up until 1971, if you had a dollar bill it represented your control of a certain amount of gold that was held by the U.S. government. It is what is referred to as the Gold Standard. Nowadays the dollar bill is a paper note representing an investment of confidence in the U.S. economy. It's still a paper asset – just indexed in a different asset.

When you invest in businesses, you can buy a part of the business or all the business. You can invest in real estate by buying the actual real estate, or you can invest in the paper version, and the paper version is always indexed in something.

The paper notes by itself isn't worth anything, but it represents your ownership in something - it's indexed. An index is something that represents your ownership in an investment area, and stocks, bonds, and mutual funds are usually indexed in businesses.

Real estate paper assets examples are tax liens, deeds, and seller finance notes on real estate properties. Seller finance notes give you control of a property if the person living in or using it isn't paying their bill. And you can own that real estate, through paper, without having to and visit the property.

You can also own paper investments in commodities. There are funds that combine a budget of things such as coffee, wheat, oil, or tea, – all the commodities that we use and raw materials that come out of the earth.

All these commodities are great things you can invest in, but there is one big aspect to understand when you're investing, education. You need to be educated about the investment.

> ## An investment isn't a good investment unless you really understand it.

I'm not talking about just buying mutual funds or having someone take money out of your employee paycheck every two weeks to put in your 401K; that's not actual investing. You're not going to make much more than keeping up with the rate of inflation is doing that kind of investing.

As I mentioned earlier, it is part of the "**40, 40, 40 Plan**." What I'm talking about is actual investing; investing that will build wealth. You need to get educated on what you are investing in.

If you want to invest in real estate, you need to learn how to do it first. If you're going actually to build wealth investing in real estate, stocks, commodities, or something else, learn about it! Learning is a life long journey and will make a huge difference in your life.

I was talking to a woman on the phone recently who was scared to invest in anything. She said, *"Real estate is just like the stock market. It can turn, and when it turns then, everybody loses their money."* That's not necessarily true; the people who are educated know what to do when the stock market turns.

Those who are educated understand that in the real estate market when the market is going up you invest in *Fix-N-Flip* or wholesaling – rentals. When the market turns sideways, you want to invest in the paper which means tax liens and tax deeds, among other things.

Apparently, there is a lot more to it because doing a *Fix-N-Flip* by itself requires a lot of knowledge, but understanding that simple formula mitigates your risk of losing any money if the market goes up, down, or sideways.

By getting educated and acquiring specific knowledge, you overcome those things that cause fear in uneducated investors.

> ## *It is the uneducated that invest at the wrong time.*

A big joke I've often heard is that when the 2008 market crash happened, many would say that their 401K became a 201K. That happened to many people because they weren't educated investors. They just turned their money over to somebody else and let them invest it (and lost half their money), instead of educating themselves on what to do when the market drops.

THE RULE OF 72

The **Rule of 72** is a formula that will tell you exactly how much money or how long it will take for your investment to double. The formula is 72 over the annual percentage rate of return on your investment.

$\frac{72}{.02\%}$

Let's say that you put your money in a savings account, and your savings account is getting **.02%** interest. You have a $100,000 that has taken you 10 years to save up. Using the **Rule of 72** it will take 3,600 years to double – that is to turn your one $100,000 into $200,000.

In my opinion – that's a bad investment. Inflation is at 3% - 5%, so an investment below that is cash flowing negative. I like to see my money double. In the case of this investment model, no one I will ever meet will be alive to see my investment double.

$\frac{72}{4\%}$

Let's look at your 401K that you're averaging 4% on – which is good for a 401k. If we take 72 over 4%, it will take you 18 years for your money to double. Now, let's say you invest in real estate.

When I invest in real estate, and I partner with somebody on a capital percentage (aka "debt") basis, the very least I pay them is 12%. The **Rule of 72** states that if you do that for six years, your money will double.

I very rarely use my personal money to invest. Because I put little to no money in, and I make a good amount of money on each transaction my rate of return is infinity. I have an infinity percent return, which is a great return! It's the best return, actually. It's the one you want to aim for.

Here is an important piece of advice for investing: if the proposed ROI ("Return On Investment" – the percentage that an investment will pay you) starts with a "point" don't do it. It's a bad investment.

For example, your savings account, it's not really "saving" your money because it isn't even keeping up with inflation, you're losing money by keeping it in a savings account. You always need to take that into account. If you think about that in the context of your 401K at 4% – you're breaking even.

INVEST IN YOURSELF

Figure 15: Invest in Yourself

I've talked a lot about getting an education. To clarify, I'm not necessarily talking about going to college or high school. One of my close friends and mentors is a high school dropout, and one of the most successful real estate investors I know.

I'm not advocating dropping out or not going to high school or college, but my point is that I have never been asked for my diploma or degree as a real estate investor. When I talk about getting an education in this book, I'm referring to getting an applied investor education.

I went to one seminar, one time, and learned one thing that I apply every day in my investing, and it's changed my life forever. An investor education is so important because it allows you to invest your knowledge and your mind.

> ### *Seek out the appropriate education for what you want to invest in.*

Hypothetically, if you were to lose everything – let's say you make one big mistake, and you must start from scratch – it's okay because you still have that tool; your education, and you still know how to make money.

If you've done it once, and you knew what you were doing (it wasn't just a fluke or an accident that you made money) you can do it all again.

Look at Donald Trump, probably the most famous real estate investor. He's had several bouts of bankruptcy, and started over, each time rebuilding his fortune. And it's not luck that keeps him bouncing back to the top. It's because he understands that his mind and his mindset are the true assets. He knows how to make money because he's taken the time and money to invest in his investor knowledge.

You must seek out your own investor knowledge. You must create that tool, work on it, and own it because it is your biggest asset. It's the thing that's going to allow you to make money as an investor.

Don't rely on other people who claim to be experts. If you're handing a portion of your paycheck over to someone else, who is also an employee, to invest for you, I'm of the opinion that you're making a mistake.

Investing is putting out money to be sure of getting more money back later at an appropriate rate. ~Warren Buffett

> like Mitch
Nelson &
his Class

Chapter 4

The Magic of Real Estate

The *fourth* key to **Mindset to Millionaire** is to *diversify your investments*. When people hear the words, "diversify your portfolio", they think that means instead of keeping all their stock in Apple they should also invest a little bit in Microsoft. That's not what diversify means. Chapter 3 discusses the different investment areas; spread your money and your wealth out across those investment areas.

Figure 16: Diversify your Investments

If you have all your money in stocks, then it's not diversified, regardless of how many companies your money is invested in. Entire markets can fluctuate. If the stock market fluctuates, you might be in trouble. I highly recommend investing in all the investment categories that have been discussed and learning how to do that effectively.

Personally, I like real estate. Real estate is my favorite investment area, and the reason for that is it has the most exit strategies.

For example, let's say I'm doing a *Fix-N-Flip* and for some reason, I end up being upside down on the deal, and I can't sell it. Maybe the market falls through the floor, or perhaps a water pipe breaks at the property, and I must pay $10,000 to fix it, and now there's no longer any profit in the transaction.

Instead of losing money I can just rent it out. If I rent it out for a year, and I make my $10,000 back, then I sell it, and I make my margin. That is plan B. Maybe I don't want to rent it out. Maybe I don't want to have to worry about selling it. Maybe I just want to make my margin back and then be done with it – then I can take advantage of leasing options.

There are a lot of exit strategies within real estate where you don't necessarily have to lose money. There is even room for mistakes while you go through the learning curve. If you're well educated and know what you're doing its one of the safer investment categories in my opinion.

If real estate really is something you're thinking about getting into I would highly recommend finding a mentor and an education platform. If you need help finding one, reach out to my team and me on our website or using the contact information on the back of this book.

An interesting point to think about is that you are currently investing in real estate; it just may not be your own. If you are a renter, then you're investing in someone's real estate. I have renters. I have several properties I rent out, and those renters are paying my mortgage, and in some cases even the HOA fees.

My renters probably don't think about it that way, and that is understandable, but besides paying their rent, they're also putting a little bit of money in my pocket every month and paying my mortgage.

You are investing in real estate in one way or another whether you realize it or not. I recommend real estate as an investment category so you can learn how to take the money you're spending every month anyway and turn it into an asset for yourself rather than an asset for someone else. As you start to build assets for yourself, you're going to start to build your own wealth.

Change your **Employee Mindset** to a **Wealthy Mindset**. Changing your mindset is about building your own wealth, not building someone else's. I've said this repeatedly, run your own business and invest in real estate.

You need to invest in real estate; wealth is neither made there, or it's held there. Think about that. The wealthy have their businesses and those businesses bring in money and where do they park that money? We've already established that they don't put it in savings accounts.

Wealthy Mindset people invest their money in real estate, and that real estate brings home a healthy safe return – so money is either held by real estate or made there.

There are some reasons why real estate is my preferred investment category, some of which I have touched on, but leverage is one of the main reasons. You can't get a loan against stocks, but you can borrow against a mortgage.

Let's say you have a family emergency and you need $30,000 that you don't have in your pocket because it's all wrapped up in investments and other things. You can get a mortgage on one of your rentals and take $30,000 out. You can't do that with stocks.

No bank is going to lend you money based on the stocks you have. You can leverage your real estate and get money for a family emergency.

Figure 17: Leverage Real Estate

You can also leverage the real estate you hold to acquire more real estate. Let's say the down payment to buy another rental is $30,000, and you have a rental you hold that already has approximately $50,000 of equity in it.

You can mortgage the property or get a home equity line of credit (HELOC) on it, and then take out $30,000 and buy another property.

Instead of making money monthly from one rental you can double that amount with two rentals. This is just one example of the numerous ways you can use leveraging in real estate to make money. It will be an essential part of your real estate investing education.

Over time, real estate appreciates. It may go up and down month to month, but if you look at a scale over a year or more, real estate appreciates. It's another aspect that I love about real estate.

In Chapter 2 we discussed the 300-plus tax deductions business owners have access to; real estate owners have over 400 tax deductions available to them. In fact, one of my favorite authors and mentors is also my attorney, Mark Kohler. He has a fantastic way, which he explains in his books, of how you can make money on real estate using current laws.

Doing this entirely legally, you can take deductions, and it will look like you are losing money because of things like depreciation on your property. You can depreciate it because someone is using it.

There are many other deductions you can take from a rental real estate that is making you money, but for tax purposes looks like you're losing money. You get money back at the end of the year!

You are making money on your real estate properties, getting a tax return, and it's entirely legal if you educate yourself on how to do it correctly. Do yourself a favor and check out *Mark Kohler's* books. He's good.

look him up

MASSIVE AND PASSIVE INCOME

In real estate, there is massive income, and you have passive income. Massive income is when you have a large amount of money coming in, like a *Fix-N-Flip* project. It's a one-time transaction, meaning you only get one check from the deal, but it's usually a good-sized one.

Let's say you profit $30,000 on a *Fix-N-Flip* that is a massive influx of money. Rather than going and buying a boat with it, a person with a **Wealthy Mindset** would use it as a down payment on a rental. Then that rental becomes a passive income source.

Passive income is different than large income in the sense that it is smaller amounts but frequent payments. In the case of a rental, you will receive monthly payments for as long as you rent out that property.

EQUITY

Equity is something you can build in both businesses and in real estate investments. You build equity by paying down your mortgage or loan, having income coming in, and building appreciation in the value of your business or real estate. You may buy it at a certain price, fix it up a little bit (which is called Forced Appreciation), and as the market goes up, and you force value, you build equity.

> ***Equity is kind of like free money.***

You may have bought something at face value for **$200,000**, and 10 years later it might be worth **$270,000**, just because the market went up. That's **$70,000** you get when you sell it just for owning it on top of all the rent you've collected or money you've made thus far.

Figure 18: Equity is Fantastic

For many people, real estate is the most straightforward investment to understand. The concept straight-forward and involves a fair exchange between a property owner, you, and the property user, the renter. A mentor, like myself, can teach you the tools and techniques to make your dreams come true. It all begins with shifting your mindset to a **Wealthy Mindset.**

You are continually learning of many ways to diversify and build your wealth. Real estate allows you to be creative, engage your mind, and build and live the life you've dreamed about. Real estate, when you have the necessary knowledge and experience, really can be magical.

Figure 19: Real Estate is Magical

Chapter 5

Never Spend the First Dollar

The *fifth* key to **Mindset to Millionaire** is *never spending the first dollar*. People in the **Employee Mindset** have their paycheck come in and what's the first thing they do with it? They give it to other people. They pay their rent, car payment, credit card bills, and any other expenses.

> **As they pass their money to other people, they are building everybody else's wealth.**

They have this mindset focusing on, "I've got to pay all my bills." But what they are really saying is, "I've got to build everybody else wealth before I build my own."

Figure 20: Money is not just a picture

The only money I have automatically withdrawn out of my account is investments, not bills. I know that every week a specific amount of money is going to come out to buy banknotes.

I know that every week a specific amount of money is going to come out and be transferred into a protected account where, as soon as we get enough money in that account, we will purchase a rental with it.

> *I pay myself first.*

I buy my assets first. I build my wealth first, and then I build other people's wealth because there are obligations I've made. In saying this, I'm not saying don't pay your bills. You have obligations and karma is real, so pay your bills and live up to your responsibilities, but pay yourself first.

You are the most *important* person, and you need to start living like it. This is what I mean by never spending the first dollar. Obviously, you can't go full throttle on this right out the gate, but this is something you can build towards.

Figure 21: Pay yourself first

By spending the second dollar on your obligations and investing the first one, you're building more and more wealth. And as your investments grow you may get to a point where you're making $20,000, $30,000, $100,000 a month.

Watch for the day when you start spending the fourth or fifth dollars on your obligations and the first, second, and third dollars are the ones you invest. That's how mega-millionaires and billionaires are made.

The **Wealthy Mindset** person understands the velocity of not spending the first dollar, and in a lot of cases they reinvest most of the money that comes back in, and it exponentiates.

One of the things you want to understand, just kind of touching back on real estate, and as I mentioned it's my favorite investment area, you can decide one time that will pay you for the rest of your life. Where else can you do that?

There are not stocks that work that way; there is not an investment that works the same way. You can decide to buy a rental tomorrow, and for the rest of your life, that structure will pay you cash flow every month.

Figure 22: Guy who gave first dollar

Chapter 6

Leverage and Good Debt VS Bad Debt

The *sixth* key of **Mindset to Millionaire** is *Leverage*. To start this chapter off, it's important to clarify the difference between an *asset* and *liability*. An asset is something that makes you money, and a liability is something that costs you money.

Assets are not free. They do cost money to purchase initially, but they will always make you more money than you pay for them.

> **Assets make you money. Liabilities cost you money.**

Liabilities, on the other hand, are things you buy that cost you money, but will never return the money you originally invested in it.

Figure 23: Difference between Bad Debt and Good Debt

There are many out there who occasionally confuse liabilities for assets. Some people will tell you their personal car is an asset. While it is true that your car is an item of value, it will rarely sell for more than you bought it for. Nor will it make you money monthly. Quite the opposite, in fact – it costs you money.

You pay for insurance, gas, tolls, your car payment, maintenance, etc. every single month, and yet the average person receives no direct income from their personal vehicle.

Some may argue that it gets them to their job, but your car isn't the one working – you are. And isn't it true that there is probably a form of public transportation you could take to get there? *Your car is a liability.*

Those same people would probably tell you that your house is an asset as well. I'm here to tell you that it is a liability. For most people, their home costs them money monthly, without putting a cent in their pocket month to month.

Again, insurance, maintenance, mortgage payments, etc. consistently cost money without returning income. Some might think their house is appreciating. True, but you probably have a mortgage, and your mortgage is amortized over 30 years to charge you somewhere around double the amount you borrowed. Don't believe me? Look at the amortization table your lending statement.

You will end up paying $600,000 - $640,000 over the 30-year term for a house on which you only borrowed $300,000. *Your house is not an asset.*

If you have a mortgage on a rental home that is making you more money that you are paying, then that is an asset.

Your mortgage, interest, taxes, and insurance cost you $800 per month, and your tenant pays you $1000 per month. Your cash flow is *$200!* That is an asset because it is netting you money (cash flow) at the end of the month.

BAD DEBT

Leverage – the difference between debt that makes you money (*good debt*) and debt that costs you money (*bad debt*). Let's talk about *bad debt* first. *Bad debt* is something you purchase on credit that does not make you money.

Figure 24: Bad Debt

If you were to purchase a big screen TV to put in your basement, what's that going to profit you? Nothing. How about a boat or water skiing equipment, what's that going to make you? Again, nothing. You just want it because it's fun.

We leverage these things, and we leverage ourselves and our time for these things. If you buy a $2,000 big screen TV or a $40,000 boat on credit, you are leveraging time you have yet to put in at your job to buy something that will depreciate over time. We call these items *liabilities*. You're buying all these things on credit and, in a way; you're choosing to rent instead of own. *Liabilities* fall into the *bad debt* category.

There are a lot of good mentors who can teach you how to get out of **bad debt.** Unfortunately, debt is something that most people in the United States, or in first world countries, face. There are so many people who have *bad debt* that our economy kind of depends on it, which isn't great, but it's a fact.

Many years ago, my wife and I listened to Dave Ramsey's Radio Show to get out of *bad debt*. He has some good systems in place for eliminating *bad debt*, and I think he offers a great place to start for most people. Get out of *bad debt*.

It will suck up your cash flow and cost you a fortune in interest if you don't. In short, *bad debt* is a debt you entered to purchase liabilities. *Liabilities are things that will never make you money.*

GOOD DEBT

Good debt is a debt that makes you money. *Good debt* is a debt that purchases assets. For example, if you have $100,000 to invest, you can either buy one $100,000 house, or you can put 20% down on 5 homes that cost $100,000 each and get 5 mortgages.

If that house is rented for $1,000 per month, you will make $1,000 per month if you put all $100,000 into one rental property.

> # Don't put all your eggs in one basket.

why ym
follow strat
Corbin?

That one house is either **100%** occupied, or **0%** occupied, and that investment can be either an asset (making you money) or liability (costing you money) a month to month, depending on whether it is rented.

On the other hand, if you split that money up into 5 down payments of $20,000 each and get $80,000 worth of mortgages on 5 properties with payments of $700 each, you will have a $300 cash flow per property. That's a total profit of $1,500 ($300x5=$1,500) per month on the same $100,000 we used in the first example.

The other benefit is you have spread out your risk of vacancies. In this strategy, 2 of your properties could be vacant all the time, and you'd still make money. You still invested $100,000. The difference was you leveraged the bank – meaning you used the bank to help spread out your risk, which in turn made you more money with less risk.

The second example above is an excellent example of good investing. An educated investor understands that *good debt* is good, and that you can leverage other people's money (including the banks') to lower your risk and increase your profit. Leveraging is part of smart investing.

Good debt is worth what you pay every month to service it because it's going to make you more money in the long run. **Good debt** stays "**good**" if you're responsible for it, but if you don't know how to invest wisely then, it can quickly turn itself into **bad debt**.

One way to make sure you're protecting yourself against all these contingencies is to make sure you're building a good investor education.

As I mentioned before, invest in yourself, get the relevant education, hire a coach or a mentor, and prepare yourself so you will be successful. We are going to talk more about where and how you can find courses and people willing to coach you in the next chapter.

> ## *Understanding good debt is to understand the power of another people's money.*

When I invested in my first house, I used **100%** of another people's money. I had arranged terms with the investor ahead of time, so his return was set. He made **12%** on the deal. I put $0 out of my own pocket into the deal, so (as I mentioned before) I received an infinite return.

Because you cannot figure a percentage based on a positive profit with $0 invested, that return is expressed as "infinity percent" or "infinite return."

BUILDING CREDIT

I've touched on a couple of different institutions for debt. There is commercial debt, which encompasses your mortgages, credit cards, installment loans, and those types of debt. Then there's non-commercial lending, which is borrowing someone else's money to invest it.

Any time you borrow from an institution, whether it's for a car or to get a mortgage on a rental property, they're going to look at your financial information. They're going to look at your credit, employment status, the amount of money you make, and they're going to take all these things into account as they're deciding whether to lend to you.

I tend to prefer non-institutionalized lending, partly because when I borrow money to do a deal I am never asked about my credit score. Nor do investors care about my personal financial situation. They simply look at the plan I have for their money. All I must do is explain to them why a given deal is a good one, and if it makes sense to them, they lend me the money.

Figure 25: Debt

There are also cases when I have used institutionalized loans; one example was a real estate rental. In real estate, it is a good thing to understand credit and what to do and not do when it comes to investing.

Many other authors are much more qualified to speak on this than I am, but I can give you the basics on good credit. When building credit, you want to make sure you have a little bit of each credit category: real estate, installment loans, and revolving credit.

Installment loans encompass loans such as a car loan, where you receive a specific amount for the car and then once it is paid off the account closes, and you must refinance if you want more money from it.

Revolving credit is any line of credit or credit card where you have a maximum balance you can use and are only charged for what you use. I would recommend having one of each of those categories if not more. You also don't want to have your credit pulled too often.

If you are not buying a house or a car, or something that's going to build your credit, then apply for a credit card. I'm not saying apply for a credit card and then go buy a TV with it. I'm saying apply for a credit card and use it for things like the repairs on a *Fix-N-Flip* or as your buffer on your rental properties, and then pay the card off over time using your rental cash flow.

It is good to have that type of credit built so you can access it when you need it. Debt is simply a tool. It is your choice as to whether you use it as ***good debt*** or ***bad debt***.

QUICK TIPS

If you're married, I don't recommend using joint credit. The reason is that if you buy a $100,000 house together, and you have a $100,000 mortgage, it looks like $100,000 on your credit and $100,000 on your spouse's credit, which lowers your buying power. Between the two of you, it looks like $200,000 of debt when it is only $100,000.

Similarly, if you have $7,500 on a credit card you both have in your name; it looks like $15,000 of debt rather than $7,500.

> # *Joint credit decreases your ability to get additional credit.*

Together you have twice the available credit. The more debt you have, the more it lowers your credit score. As you reduce that debt, your credit score will go back up. The threshold to where it really starts to affect your credit is about 50% debt to credit ratio.

Never close a revolving credit account if possible. Closing this type of account can have a long-term negative effect on your credit score. If you have a credit card that you no longer use, then consider cutting the card up instead of closing the account. Each time you close a credit card accounts your credit score will be penalized.

If the card has an annual fee, and you don't want to be stuck with the payment, try changing to a different card program with fewer benefits, or perhaps negotiating the fee with the credit card company. Whatever you do, do your best to avoid closing the account because high credit scores are essential in many investing areas.

MISUSE OF TOOLS

I have had the heart of an entrepreneur since the beginning of my life. I started my first business at the age of seven with my best friend Jesse; it was a leaf raking business.

We printed out some homemade business cards on tractor fed printer paper and distributed them throughout the neighborhood.

At the age of 12, I took out a capital loan of $100 from my dad to buy an aerator attachment for my family's riding lawnmower. I then proceeded to canvas my neighborhood selling aeration service for $50 per yard. I was able to pay my dad back the $100 I had borrowed, as well as, retain a significant profit on top of my original investment. I probably made $300 that summer.

At the age of 15, I was in the ninth grade. I had moved to a new school and made new friends. My closest friend Nick and I had a keen interest in personal computers. We learned how to build them by disassembling and reassembling my family's computer.

We learned all about software and the operating systems of the era. We became intimately familiar with each piece of hardware: RAM memory, the CPU (Which at the time were only single core), the motherboard, the power supply, and any other necessary components.

As we got more and more familiar with these components, we started to realize that building a computer was actually very simple. Every component had a specific place on the motherboard; most components would only fit into the appropriate ports, so there wasn't much room for error.

We learned which component brands worked best together and the software optimization to make them perform well. We decided, being of entrepreneurial minds, that we could make a fortune (in our minds) by building computers for people in our neighborhood. We would buy the components from the local computer supply store, mark them up, and charge for our services as well.

This became quite the profitable business for Nick and me. We made several hundred dollars per machine. My best guess is we sold 20 machines that year.

In addition to building the machines and selling them, we also gained a reputation as the computer experts of the neighborhood. Anyone who had issues with their personal computers would call us, and we would serve them at an hourly rate.

Not a bad business for a couple of 15-year-olds! Spending our time on something creative and constructive also probably kept us out of the kinds of trouble most 15-year-olds get into. I was never interested in being rebellious.

> *My passion has always lied in creating businesses and business systems and making those systems successful.*

Nick and I rarely received calls to service computers that we built, but every now and then we would get a call on a faulty part.

One call sticks out in my mind. Nick called me laughing one afternoon and told me he had been the victim of a prank call from a customer of ours. A woman in the neighborhood who had us build a computer for her several months earlier called Nick one afternoon. "My cup holder is broken," she said, "Cup holder?" Nick asked "Yeah, my cup holder is broken. It won't go back in." She replied.

It took some back and forth, but eventually, Nick figured out that she was referring to her CD-ROM drive. She had allegedly been using the CD loading tray as an automated coaster for her beverage. It came out later that the woman had staged the call based on an article she had read in a tech magazine. Several similar stories, apparently true, have been recanted in various publications.

I tell this story because it illustrates an important point: it is human nature to misuse tools if we do not understand them. Someone, somewhere, at some point in time, thought that a retractable CD-ROM loading tray was there as a convenient place to rest his or her $.50 soda. The misuse of that item made it significantly less valuable.

A device that was designed to allow its owner access to limitless libraries of information with an unlimited potential for knowledge and learning, or consumption of the arts, was reduced to a mere shelf for a 12-ounce can of cola.

Could you imagine seeing a power drill for the first time if you had no point of reference, no context and no idea what it was used for? Or, what would you think of a screw if you didn't know what a drill or a screwdriver was? Maybe it would appear to you as an odd nail. You might use a hammer to try to drive a screw into the wood. It would be a bit of a disaster.

I know that sounds preposterous, but people in the **Employee Mindset** do things like that every day. They do things like storing their money in savings accounts that yield them 0.01% to 0.02% when they have an amortized mortgage loan on their house or their car.

They look at a **6%** mortgage that will cost them **$640,000** over 30 years on **$300,000** borrowed and think that that is cheaper than the 21% line of credit that is non-amortized simple interest. When they get the chance, they refinance the non-amortized line balance into the amortized loan.

To adequately explain why this is a problem, it's important to understand the right banking tools. Once you understand these tools, you'll have an advantage over 99% of your peers, who think as described above.

When we're young, most of us go down to the bank with our parents to set up a checking and savings account. We're taught that as we make money, we should store it in our checking account, so we have easy access to it to pay our bills monthly. If there is any surplus at the end of the month, we are taught to put it into our savings account to create buying power.

That buying power will be necessary in the case of an emergency. What if we need to fix our car? What if we have unexpected medical bills? It will be nice to have those savings there to be able to pay for those things when they come up, right?

Employees are so focused on the amount of money they make. "I make $3,500 a month," "I make $120,000 a year," or "I make $50 an hour." The problem is if they spend the same amount they make, they're broke – regardless of how big or little their income is.

> ## The Wealthy Mindset rarely talks about what they "make."

They don't really care; it's irrelevant to them. The wealthy focus on cash flow, which simply put, is income minus expenses. If you make $3,500 a month, spend $1,000 on your mortgage, $500 on your car payment, $300 on credit card payments, $1,200 on living expenses, and put the $500 left over in savings you've segmented your money and have nothing left over to invest. That's a cash flow of zero.

Because there's nothing left over at the end of the month, the average American must put surprise expenses on their credit card. When the payment gets to be more than they can bear, they refinance their house and consolidate their credit card debt into their house payment, thinking they're trading a higher interest rate for a lower one. This couldn't be further from the truth.

If I were to say that water freezes at 32°, would that be an accurate statement?

If you said yes, you're right and also wrong. If you said yes, it's because you assumed, I was referring to the Fahrenheit scale. But what if I was referring to the Celsius scale? Then you would've been wrong.

Freshwater does freeze at 32° Fahrenheit at sea level. That same freezing point is also measured at 0° Celsius. The point at which water freezes didn't change, the scale with which I measured it did.

Would you rather pay 6% on a mortgage or 21% on a credit card or line of credit? Guess what? They're not measured on the same scale.

There are two categories of lending instruments that banks use: *loans* and *lines of credit*. *Loans* are one-directional, meaning when you put money in you can't easily take it back out. When you pay your mortgage, you can't go to the grocery store that same day and use your mortgage to buy groceries.

However, **lines of credit** are two directional. You can pay your credit card payment and on the same day use it to buy groceries, put gas in your car, and pay your utilities. Because of those fundamental differences, banks calculate interest differently for the two distinct categories.

> ## *Keep in mind a bank is a business.*

They want to make as much money off you as possible. That's not a bad thing; it's just business. Because loans are one directional, they can create an amortization schedule that front-end loads all the interest they will be charging you over the life of the loan.

Let's say that hypothetically your mortgage payment is $1,000. If you were to look at the amortization schedule on this hypothetical loan, you would see that something like $950 goes to interest, and $50 goes to the principal with the first payment.

That means $50 is all that goes towards paying the bank back for the money they lent you. The other $950 goes directly into their pocket, never to be seen by you again.

As you make the payments on your mortgage over 30 years, the balance shifts the other direction. Your 360^{the} payment would show something along the lines of $950 going to principle and $50 going to interest. It seems like it will all balance out in the end, right? Wrong.

> ### *The average American refinances their mortgage every seven years.*

That means the average American pays the front-end loaded interest portion of their mortgage in a seven-year cycle for their entire lives.

Most **lines of credit** cannot be front-end loaded with interest because **lines of credit** are two directional. You can make the payment and on the same day spend money out of the line. Interest, in many cases, works differently and must be calculated daily.

This daily interest is added up over 30 days, and that amount becomes your credit card payment. Some lending institutions also add a little bit of principal payment requirement to the monthly bill. Nevertheless, if you have *$50* in principal at *21%* (this is the annual interest rate), you will pay $0.88 in interest the first month.

Let's compare the two:

	Principal in Month 1	Interest Paid in Month 1	Effective Annual Interest Rate
Line of Credit *(Credit Card, Simple Unamortized Interest)*	$50.00	$0.88	21%
Loan *(Mortgage, Amortized Interest)*	$50.00	$950.00	22,800%

Figure 26: Example Amortization Schedule

Which would you rather pay? Now, I know this isn't an actual example of an actual amortization schedule for a real mortgage, but look at your mortgage. It's in your truth-in-lending statement that you got at closing on your house. This example isn't far off, and the principle is valid.

We're told credit cards, and *lines of credit* are evil, and we believe it. I just showed you how credit cards are a thousand percent better for you monthly than your mortgage.

This is an excellent example of how the **Employee Mindset** can hurt you.

After all of this, will you ever be tempted to refinance your house to consolidate your credit cards again?

I hope not. This is how the wealthy see lending tools. It's not that one is evil, and one is good, they're just tools. It's important that we understand what they are and how to use them.

Therefore, your investor education is so important! Get educated before you go out and start taking out mortgages on rentals thinking you're a savvy investor.

Figure 27: Debt Categories

Chapter 7

Education

The *seventh* key to **Mindset to Millionaire** is *education*. If you want to financially successful, you must obtain the education necessary to invest correctly.

Figure 28: Education

Before we discuss the importance of *education* in changing your mindset, I want to tell you a story.

THE PONZI SCHEME

Several years ago, I was invited to join a lucrative "investment" opportunity. At the time, I was an uneducated investor eager to get onto the investing scene. A friend of mine named Kyle approached me one night and told me he and his father had invested a lot of money into a program that purchased American made vehicles for evaluation.

He told me the program needed funding so they could purchase vehicles from manufacturers to give to drivers for a period in exchange for an evaluation of the vehicle on a quarterly basis.

The idea was that the financial backers would purchase the vehicles for cash or finance them. The monthly return was supposed to be enough to cover any monthly payment plus a significant amount of profit – interest paid monthly, calculated at 48% per year.

Kyle then told me he was making money doing it as well as driving a brand new, fancy, shiny car.   Feigning to be an intelligent investor, I asked as many questions as I could think of. It turned out this was all run by a single person – we'll call her, Nancy.

Nancy apparently had negotiated a deal with the three major American automobile manufacturers that would fetch a significant fee for each evaluation the drivers in this program produced. I remember the whole thing at the time seemed too good to be true, but I was eager to invest, and I was excited by the thought of driving an excellent new car. I was a dumb, uneducated investor.

What did my dumb, uneducated investor mind think? Of course, I thought this was a good idea! "I get a new car?!" "And I'm going to make money on top of it?!" "This would turn my car into an asset instead of a liability!" I approached that investment entirely on emotion.

Excited to get started with this new get-rich opportunity, I took the $10,000 I had in savings down to their office and handed it over. Also, I financed two top-of-the-line Fords as evaluation vehicles, each costing about $60,000. For those who are counting, that's a total of $130,000 invested.

As if that weren't enough, I convinced my dad to finance another $120,000 worth of vehicles for the evaluation program. Before I knew it, I was responsible for quarter million dollars being dumped into this program that I had qualified based on emotion only.

The first month went by, and I received the payments for my vehicles as well as the additional interest I was promised. The next month, I was told money was a little tight, so they would only have to pay the interest for that month, but it would not be a problem in the future.

For a few months after that, the payments on my vehicles were made, but the additional interest owed to me was not paid. Only six short months after starting the program, I noticed that one of the car payments had gone unpaid.

A couple weeks later I received a notice that the second car payment hadn't been paid. I called Nancy's office and inquired as to the late payment notice. They said they were working on getting the money together, and I would be paid shortly– not to worry.

Nervously, I did as they instructed. My wife and I scrounged up enough money to make both $1000 for each car payment that month. It was only a few weeks later that I received a phone call from Kyle. He informed me that earlier that day Nancy had been arrested by the FBI.

It turned out the whole thing was a Ponzi scheme. To add insult to injury, it came to light that this was not the first time Nancy had been caught doing something like this. I had lost my $10,000. I was left holding the bag for $120,000 in car payments, and I was responsible for getting my dad into the same situation.

Even before I knew the investment was a fraud, I didn't consider that the investment had a major linchpin – Nancy. She played things very close to the chest. She didn't tell anyone who her contacts were, her employees had no idea how to run the business if something were to happen to her, and all the financial backers relied on her and her connections to get paid.

The major problem with this investment was that I, as the investor, had no control. This wasn't a hard asset I was investing in, it was a relationship. Not only that, it was a relationship I had no part in. I invested a significant amount of money into the relationship between Nancy – a person I had only met a couple times, and her "contacts" whom I'd never met.

There was no asset I was investing in. The cars were not making me money; it was the relationship that was allegedly making me money. A relationship is not one of the investment criteria we talked about in Chapter 3: business, real estate, or commodities.

It was not an investment in business because I was not receiving ownership in the business for my investment. And it was obviously not an investment in real estate or commodities.

Even if the program had not been a Ponzi scheme, it would have been a bad investment because I had no control. It doesn't matter if Nancy had guaranteed me 48% interest per year, 148% interest per year, or 1480% interest per year.

> ### *It was a bad investment because it relied solely on someone else.*

At the time, as an uneducated investor, 48% per year seemed like a lot to me. I didn't know of any other investment that could possibly yield that much.

Thanks to my investor education, I make investments that yield an infinite return for me and returns in the hundreds of percent annually for my partners.

I can do this with assets that I have complete control of usually based on real estate. I make the decisions. If I want to buy a property, I buy a property. If I want to sell a property, I sell the property. If I want to keep it and rent it out, I do it. I'm in control, and I call the shots.

I have kept in touch with Kyle. We are still good friends. He mentioned to me the other day that he felt bad for getting me into the Ponzi scheme mess. I told him I didn't blame him, and I don't. It was my fault for thinking I could navigate such a complicated investment as an uneducated investor.

In some ways, I'm grateful for the opportunity to have experienced that. Don't get me wrong, it was a huge burden for my wife and me to overcome; but it taught me a great lesson: never invest in anything I can't control. I consider that experience a huge part of my investor education. *I will never make a similar mistake again.*

The classes and mentoring I eventually sought out and purchased were significantly less expensive than what that lesson cost me. I only spent about $20,000 on those classes, and what I have taken away from the classes has returned much, much more to me than the original investment.

My experience with Nancy will never provide me any kind of monetary return though it may save me from making similar mistakes in the future.

> ## *As an investor, you can't be scared to fail.*

As I mentioned before, failure is a stepping stone. Had I not failed with that investment, I may not have been motivated to seek out my investor education. Had that not happened, I wouldn't have written this book. I may not even have been an investor at this point.

With that said, you can avoid these kinds of pitfalls by starting your investor career with a proper investor education. An investor education is not something you will find in a public school or accredited university. It's usually something done on a smaller scale that you have to seek out.

The Ponzi scheme story is part of my motivation for extending my career as an investor into that of a mentor. I am passionate about helping others get an education in investing, so they don't have to make some of the same mistakes I made starting out.

Figure 29: Knowledge is Power

The more you know through education, the more you will be able to control the outcome and change to a ***Wealthy Mindset*** and become financially secure.

NO MORE EXCUSES

Often, I think people approach education like it's too late for them, saying, "I am 50, what could they possibly teach me that I don't already know?" or "Maybe I should have done this 20 years ago." You might be right, maybe the best time to have done it was twenty years ago, but my question is, "When is the second-best time to do it?"

The answer is RIGHT NOW!!

I'm part of an investment community, and in that community, there are people of all ages. There are people younger than me. I turn 30 next year, and there are people younger than me – significantly younger than me. There are people in their late teens in these investing communities, people in their 70s, and everybody in between. I work with people of all ages.

It is never too late! It's never too late to start building true wealth. You're only going to do that through education, though. What I can tell you is regardless of where you are at in life; you don't have enough time or money to try to figure it out on your own.

There are too many ways for things to go wrong. There too many elements – too many ways for it to fail and not enough ways for it to go right for you to be able to "wing it." You'll spend a lot less time and a lot less money if you get an education.

If you don't feel comfortable asking your grandmother to lend you her life savings so you can invest in real estate and make her return, then you're not ready to invest in real estate. You need to get an education. If you do, you will get to a point where you feel comfortable moving grandma's money from a low-interest bank account or CD and investing it.

With education and experience, you'll be able to make her money while understanding the risks. You will also understand how to avoid those risks and know how to invest her life savings appropriately.

Some of the other obstacles that might be holding you back are time, money, credit, or lack of knowledge. What I hear when people tell me about these challenges is that they are afraid. Fear is usually the biggest reason people hold themselves back. I can tell you all those concerns, and any others you might have can be overcome with education.

> ## *Fear is the lack of knowledge.*

Fear is the opposite of knowledge and can be overcome with understanding. The more you learn about something and the more experience you have, the less fear you will experience. All the objections listed above, and any others you could use as an excuse for why you can't be an investor, are not good enough.

You can be an investor, you just need an education. The return you get on your education will be much more than any other investment you ever make.

> **Knowledge is the tool that enables you to change your mindset.**

Mindset is the key to changing your life. Contact me at the email below, or visit my website, and let's get you started in your next phase in life as an investor! I want to mentor you on your way to success by introducing you to the best people and education available.

Figure 30: Education

About the Author

 For over 10 years, Mitch Nelson has enjoyed starting, running and investing in businesses and real estate. Like many of his companies, he has thrived in business taking on each new challenge it brings. From the printing industry to service and retail, as well as information and technology companies, Mitch's portfolio of influence as an entrepreneur is well known throughout the Rocky Mountain region. His hands-on experience in many corners of business is a trusted resource for his colleagues and investors alike.

One of Mitch's most exciting business ventures has been that of real estate investing. With his years of experience, he's learned to navigate and make money in the real estate realm while learning to avoid pitfalls and traps that claim many young investors. He has dedicated much of his time to teaching others his techniques and passing on his secrets of the industry through writing, videos, coaching and education programs. Contact Mitch A. Nelson at:

Email: mitchanelson@gmail.com

Web: www.MitchANelson.com

To get updates on this book and access a FREE Millionaire Mindset Checklist text your Name and Email to

1 (801) 666-4776

or visit

www.MitchANelson.com.

You can also schedule a consulting session with Mitch Nelson.

60591526R00085

Made in the USA
Columbia, SC
17 June 2019